CONQUERING YOUR GIANTS

BIBLICAL STRATEGIES TO CONQUER WHAT'S BEEN CONQUERING YOU

A BIBLE STUDY IN JOSHUA

PAT J. SIKORA

Pat J. Sikora - Mighty Oak Ministries
Sugar Land, Texas

CONQUERING YOUR GIANTS
Biblical Strategies to Conquer What's Been Conquering You
Copyright © 1986, 1989, 1995, 2012, 2021, 2023, 2024 by Pat J. Sikora
All Rights Reserved.

ISBN 978-1-947877-08-5 paperback
ISBN 978-1-947877-09-2 ebook

Library of Congress Control Number

Cover and Interior Design: Jbookdesigns@josepepito
Cover Background Design: ID 319838198 © Iftikhar Alam | Dreamstime.com
Cover Concept: Arloa Gundred

No portion of this book may be reproduced for any purpose without the author's written permission.
Published in the United States of America.
Unless otherwise noted, all Scripture quotations are from the New King James Version®. Copyright © 1982 by Thomas Nelson. Used by permission. All rights reserved.

Scripture quotations identified as ESV are from the ESV® Bible (The Holy Bible, English Standard Version®), © 2001 by Crossway, a publishing ministry of Good News Publishers. Used by permission. All rights reserved.

Scripture quotations identified as KJV are from The Authorized (King James) Version. Rights in the Authorized Version in the United Kingdom are vested in the Crown. Reproduced by permission of the Crown's patentee, Cambridge University Press.

Scripture quotations marked (NIV) are taken from the Holy Bible, New International Version®, NIV®. Copyright © 1973, 1978, 1984, 2011 by Biblica, Inc.™ Used by permission of Zondervan. All rights reserved worldwide. www.zondervan.com The "NIV" and "New International Version" are trademarks registered in the United States Patent and Trademark Office by Biblica, Inc.™

For more resources and free downloads, go to:
Website: www.PatSikora.com
Facebook: Facebook.com/mightyoakministries
Email: Pat@PatSikora.com
Youtube: Pat Sikora

DEDICATION

This book is lovingly dedicated to my son,

Joshua Paul,

whose birth and name inspired me to study the book of Joshua. I'm so proud of the man you've become and the giants you've already conquered. May you conquer many more in your lifetime, through the power of Jesus Christ.

WITH GRATITUDE

A book doesn't write itself, and it's seldom a one-person process. I am indebted to so many people who helped make this dream a reality.

My friend Sandra Meyer poured over every page, sometimes repeatedly, to edit and copy-edit it. My critique group lovingly held me to the highest standard, just as they have with my other books. Thank you, Darla Bennet, Laurie Kehler, and Stephanie Shoquist. In addition to the above, who regularly prayed for me, I'm grateful to Sheridan Jones for praying me through and cheering me on.

A special thanks to Jose Pepito, who patiently and professionally designed both the interior and cover, as he has done for several of my books.

And most of all, I'm grateful to my LORD and Savior, Jesus Christ, the Commander of Heaven's Armies (Jehovah Sabaoth), who has led me in many giant-killing battles and taught me the skills I now share with you.

CONTENTS

A NOTE FROM PAT ix

LEADERS! BEFORE YOU BEGIN xi

EVERYONE BEFORE YOU BEGIN xiii

CHAPTER 1
PREPARING TO CONQUER 1

CHAPTER 2
TRAINING IN LIFE'S BOOT CAMP 19

CHAPTER 3
CONQUERING FEAR 37

CHAPTER 4
OVERCOMING OBSTACLES 55

CHAPTER 5
DEMOLISHING STRONGHOLDS 71

CHAPTER 6
LEARNING TO WAIT 85

CHAPTER 7
FACING THE CONSEQUENCES **99**

CHAPTER 8
WINNING GOD'S WAY. **113**

CHAPTER 9
DUPED BY DECEPTION **125**

CHAPTER 10
CONFRONTING A GANG OF GIANTS **141**

CHAPTER 11
TAKING THE OFFENSIVE **155**

CHAPTER 12
FACING CHANGE **171**

CHAPTER 13
FINISHING WELL **189**

APPENDIX A
FEARS THAT CONQUER ME. **207**

APPENDIX B
TRANSFORMING NEGATIVE THOUGHTS (TNT)™ . . . **213**

BIBLIOGRAPHY. **219**

A NOTE FROM PAT

Are you tired of Bible studies that insult your intelligence with questions that have obvious answers or are merely academic?

Are you tired of Bible studies that don't prod you to go deeper with the Lord or address your deepest needs?

I was too. That's why I started writing Bible studies. But here's what I've found.

My Bible studies are NOT for everyone.

No, I'm not trying to discourage you before you begin, but I do want you to recognize that *Conquering Your Giants* is not your average Bible study.

So, who is this study **NOT** for?

- *First, it's not for you if you have no problems.* Or if you have problems (giants) that you aren't interested in conquering at this point in your life. That's OK. It may not be your season. But don't buy this book if everything in your life is OK.

- *Second, it's not for you if you're in a hurry.* This study is longer than most because giant conquering is likely to take a while. You know that. Big goals take time. If you aren't willing or able to give it the time it needs, this may not be your season. And that's OK.

- ***Third, it's not for you if you can't invest the time to do the work.*** This is not a study where you can just show up on Wednesday night and see your friends. It's a study that requires a couple of hours per week in addition to your group meeting. And it requires you to dig deep and be honest with yourself and your group. If you don't do the work, you simply won't reap the benefits. If you can't invest the time, it may not be your season. And that really is OK.

So, who **IS** this study for?

- ***It's for anyone who has a "giant" in their life that has become a big enough problem that you know it's time to address it.*** Something you just haven't been able to conquer despite your best efforts. A giant that is keeping you from being transformed to the image of Christ (2 Corinthians 3:18).

- ***It's for anyone who's willing to invest the time to not just wound their giant but conquer it once and for all.*** This study is designed for real transformation. And real transformation doesn't happen overnight or even in six weeks. It takes time to conquer a giant, just like it took Joshua time to conquer the Promised Land. This study is designed for 13 weeks. Many groups find they want to take longer.

- ***It's for anyone who is willing to seriously do the work*** and prayerfully take their giant before the Lord with the intent of conquering once and for all.

So the question is: Is this study for you? If so, let's get started! I'm praying for you and would love to hear about your progress. And your success.

Pat Sikora

Pat@PatSikora.com

LEADERS! BEFORE YOU BEGIN

First, thank you for being willing to lead this study. I know you'll learn more and appreciate it more because you've made that investment.

Second, please know that this study is designed so that you are not a *teacher*. You're a *facilitator*. The study is self-propelling. If group members do the work, you don't have to. Your job is to facilitate, to keep the discussion moving, and to make sure that everyone gets to participate.

Third, to help you with this important job, we've provided you with a *free* Leader's Guide. Just click the QR code below to access it. We've tried to anticipate questions that you or your group may have and provided additional information to help you out.

Fourth, we're here to help. There are many leadership resources at PatSikora.com, especially on the Branches and Roots sections. If you run into a problem, you can reach out to me at Pat@PatSikora.com. My goal is to make you look good!

I would love your feedback. How can we make this study even better? And if you love the study, please leave a review on Amazon. Reviews are so important to getting the word out about new products. Thanks in advance!

Pat Sikora

EVERYONE BEFORE YOU BEGIN

Frequently Asked Questions

What's the Best Way to Do This Study? Group or Alone?

Conquering Your Giants is designed for small groups, but it can also be done alone. Let me share some caveats for each choice.

Small Group

You'll gain maximum benefit from this study by doing it with others. **HOWEVER, this is not a drop in study.** It's a study designed to conquer whatever has been conquering you, and that's not casual Wednesday night conversation. It's serious business. You don't want strangers or people who haven't been tracking with you suddenly appearing when you're in the middle of a stuck point or an obstacle. You want those with whom you've developed a close, confidential relationship. Those with whom you have developed trust. It's important to stress confidentiality in your group. What's said in your group stays in your group. That will facilitate growth.

Therefore, we recommend a closed group of no more than eight people with attendance "mandatory." We ask people to make a commitment to attend because when one person is absent, they will be missed. Make this group a commitment in your schedule. For your sake and for the sake of your groupmates.

Do It Alone

Yes, you can do it alone and it can be incredibly effective. You can move at your own pace and allow the Lord to work in you in His own personal way. But let me encourage you to find at least one friend to do it with you. There are some questions where it will be easy to fool yourself. A trusted friend with permission to speak into your life can challenge you. And that hidden area might be just the thing holding your giant in place.

Use a Good Translation

To gain maximum benefit from the study, we encourage you to use a good translation of the Bible such as the *New King James Version* (NKJV), *English Standard Version* (ESV), *New International Version* (NIV), or the *Revised Standard Version* (RSV) rather than a paraphrase such as *The Message, The Good News Bible,* or *The Living Bible*. Often, reading a passage in several translations is useful to its understanding. A parallel Bible containing several translations side by side is an easy way to do this.

Do a Little Every Day

Given the nature of the questions, you'll benefit most from the study if you work on it a little each day. Most lessons have 15 to 25 questions and should take an average of two hours to complete. If you're doing the study in a small group, take the first day following your group meeting to read through the entire lesson for the next week. This will plant the questions in your mind so you can think and pray about them all week.

If your group schedule allows, you may want to divide each lesson in half and take 26 weeks rather than 13. Most groups have found that the questions generate a *lot* of discussion as group members work to conquer their giants (which you will identify in Week 2).

Then, try to spend some time each day working on the study rather than waiting until the night before your next meeting. This will provide you with at least three benefits.

1. First and most importantly, it will build a habit of consistent, daily Bible study in your life. Spending a short time in the Bible every day is more beneficial to your growth than a lengthy session once a week.

2. Second, it will allow you time to learn the memory verse, planting the topic of the study in your heart and mind through the Word of God.

3. Finally, it will allow you plenty of time to consider and implement the application questions designed to help you conquer your giant. This study focuses on application. It is serious business. Its goal is to see your life changed for Jesus Christ.

Types of Questions

In this study, you'll find four types of questions. Let's take a quick look at what they are and why they're there.

Icebreaker – Focusing

In this study, we call this "Getting Started." It's the first question in every chapter. It has two goals. First, it focuses your attention on the theme of the chapter and, in a casual, non-threatening way, draws your attention away from the hundred other distractions you face. It gets people used to hearing their own voices and the voices of others in this setting today.

Second, it's useful when the group is new to ask a nonthreatening question with no right or wrong answer. It lets you get acquainted with the other members in your group.

After your group has jelled, you'll probably decide to ignore the icebreaker during your discussion and jump right into the heart of the study. That's fine.

Observation – What does it say?

The Observation question simply asks, *"What does the text say?"* It usually has a single right answer that is clear from the passage. Observation questions are the stuff that most Bible study guides are made of, directing your attention to the Bible text to clarify what the passage says and what it doesn't say. But alone, they can be boring and even insult your intelligence.

Interpretation – What does it mean?

The interpretation question asks, *"What does the text mean?"* Interpretation questions may require some additional digging. You may need to understand the passage within the context of the book or the whole of Scripture. You may need to do a word study on a specific Greek or Hebrew expression. You may need to use a Bible dictionary or other resources to understand the cultural setting. Or you may need to synthesize the answers from two or three preceding observation questions to draw the true meaning from the text.

Interpretation questions often ask, "How?" "Why?" or "What do you think?" Observation questions, by contrast, usually ask, "What?" or "When?" Interpretation questions add a bit of meat to that white bread.

Application – Who cares?

The Application question asks, *"Who cares?"* or *"What must I do about it?"* The answer may be implied from the text, but it requires the participant to get personal. Application is where giants are killed, and people are conformed to the image of Jesus Christ. They are the key to this study. Application questions are intentionally personal and ask for a commitment. They probe feelings, motivations, and obstacles. They're pretty tough to ignore. This results in participants looking deeply enough to allow the Holy Spirit to call them to repent and change.

As you go through the study, look for all four types of questions and pay attention to how each contributes to conquering your giant.

WEEK 1
PREPARING TO CONQUER

All of our theology must eventually become biography. The constant challenge in this life we call Christian is the translation of all we believe to be true into our day-to-day lifestyle.[1]
~Tim Hansel

Have you ever felt overwhelmed by the circumstances of your life?

Have you ever experienced fear so penetrating that it caused you to turn your back on what you knew to be God's will for you?

Have you ever been careless in your obedience to God and suffered the consequences of that action?

Have you ever obeyed God by stepping into the raging torrents of life—and suddenly experienced the power of the LORD beyond your wildest imagination?

---

[1] Tim Hansel, *Ya' Gotta Keep Dancin'* (Elgin, Ill.: David C. Cook Publishing Company, 1985), 41.

If so, you have a lot in common with Joshua, the man who conquered the giants of Canaan and led God's people, the Israelites, into the Promised Land.

Over the next few months, you'll get to know the ordinary person of Joshua. Not just the character between the books of Deuteronomy and Judges, but the real person of Joshua.

The ordinary person who was overwhelmed by his responsibilities.

The ordinary person whom the LORD needed to remind again and again, "Do not be afraid; do not be terrified…"

The ordinary person who, by forgetting to seek the LORD's will, brought destruction upon his nation.

And the ordinary person who experienced the parting of the raging Jordan River as his people crossed on dry land.

If you are an ordinary person who truly wants to be used in extraordinary ways by the Lord, this study is for you!

You'll also learn a great deal about holy warfare and the giants that loom in the life of each believer in Jesus Christ. And you'll learn from the life of Joshua that God can, will, and does use ordinary people to lead extraordinary lives for Him.

Just Ordinary

Joshua was indeed an ordinary man. Born a slave, he was probably in his 40s when Moses led the Israelites in their exodus from the brick factories of Egypt. He spent the next 40 years serving as an aide to Moses. His life is often overshadowed by the more spectacular exploits of Moses and by the wilderness wanderings of his less disciplined contemporaries.

Faithful Obedience

Joshua lived a life of faithful obedience, and as obedience built upon obedience, he emerged as an extraordinary leader for the LORD his God. Author Phillip Keller describes him this way:

> *Against the background of a stubborn, stiff-necked nation moving reluctantly and in rebellion against God's will, ... this mighty man prepared to carry out God's commands at any cost. Despite the dark unbelief all around him, despite the rebellion of his people, despite the delays of forty desert years, Joshua emerges triumphant. He is the commanding character who finds his faith in God vindicated in resounding victories.[2]*
> ~W. Phillip Keller

Our Lives Look a Lot Like Joshua's

Despite the differences in time and place, our lives contain many parallels to Joshua's life and times. Therefore, we have much to learn from this man's faithful obedience.

While we might initially resist a study so full of bloody battles and gruesome warfare, a closer examination reveals its contemporary nature. The Apostle Paul suggested in 1 Corinthians 10:1-13 that Old Testament history was given to us as an example, implying that although the settings may be different, the principles are similar.

---

[2] W. Phillip Keller, *Joshua : Mighty Warrior and Man of Faith* (Grand Rapids, Mich.: Kregel Publications, 1992), 12.

Both the Old and New Testaments affirm that each believer is regularly engaged in battle, not "against flesh and blood, but against principalities, against powers, against the rulers of the darkness of this age, against spiritual *hosts* of wickedness in the heavenly *places*" (Ephesians 6:12).

Because of this, all believers are commanded to "put on the full armor of God" (Ephesians 6:13-18), not so they can piously sit in the pews, but so they can stand firmly in the face of the enemy and so that, having stood, they may emerge victorious.

Getting Topical

The book of Joshua is a narrative historical portion of Scripture that tells the story of the Israelites' entry into and conquest of the Promised Land. As New Testament believers, we can draw a variety of lessons and principles from this narrative. In this study, however, we'll focus on only *one* topical approach to the book—that of *conquering giants*.

This approach is certainly not the only one that could be used. Indeed, an inductive study of Joshua would produce many lessons and principles not related to conquering giants. On the other hand, the topic of conquering giants is central to the whole of the book, so this approach is not irresponsible.

Therefore, remember that this is a topical study. While we'll practice good exegesis of the text, whenever possible, we'll relate it to conquering our giants. In test groups, this approach has produced life-changing and lasting impacts on each reader's life.

Conquering Giants

To apply the topical approach, we'll use symbolism throughout the study. The two symbols most frequently used are *"giants"* and *"promised land."*

The spies in Numbers 13:33 used the term "giants" to describe the inhabitants of the Promised Land. Some of these inhabitants, especially the Anakim, were literal, physical giants who vigorously fought to maintain control of what they considered to be their land.

After a dramatic exodus from the slave pits of Egypt, a miraculous Red Sea crossing, and a two-year journey led by God Himself, the Israelites reached the edge of the Promised Land. Moses, exercising due diligence, sent twelve men across the border to spy out the land. Returning after 40 days in Canaan, ten of those spies reported in fear to Moses,

> The land through which we have gone as spies is a land that devours its inhabitants, and all the people whom we saw in it are men of great stature. There we saw the giants (the descendants of Anak came from the giants); and *we were like grasshoppers in our own sight, and so we were in their sight* (Numbers 13:32-33, emphasis mine).

Their negative report caused the Israelites to quake in fear and to refuse to go in and conquer the land God had already promised them. As a result, the nation was sentenced to wander in the wilderness for 40 years.

Ironically, after 40 years of wandering, they still had to face these same giants—but the giants had become even more powerful, more sophisticated, and more deeply entrenched in the land.

I've Got Giants, and So Do You

You and I also face giants. And we also must make a choice. We will either go in and conquer those giants, thus inheriting our promised land[3]—or we will refuse to conquer them and, like the Israelites, be relegated to a period of wilderness wandering, which will only postpone the inevitable need to face them.

> *God is gracious. He'll allow you to wander as long as you choose to.*

Just what are our giants? They can be any number of things, depending on each person's spiritual and personal development. For example:

1) A giant may be an *attitude, behavior, or sin* that is keeping you from enjoying a victorious, joyful Christian life or, in the terms of this study, from inheriting your promised land. This giant might be a sinful attitude that doesn't glorify the LORD, such as fear,[4] pride, unbelief, anger, bitterness, envy, strife, discouragement, depression, or a critical spirit. Or it may be a sinful behavior such as lying, cheating, gossiping, pornography, addiction, or adultery. Your giant may be any sin, behavior, or emotion you can't seem to conquer on your own.

2) A giant may be a *real problem* in your life—the lack of a job, a difficult relationship, problems with children, unbelieving relatives, an illness, or weight you can't seem to lose… It may be a decision you need to make—to get married, get pregnant, take that job, move to Texas… These giants may seem insurmountable to you. As you study, you may find that some of the attitudes or behaviors listed above contribute to the success of that giant—and to your seeming inability to conquer it.

3) If you have those two areas well under control, your giant may be a *call from the LORD* that you would rather ignore. Perhaps you feel a call to take a greater role

---

[3] More about this in a few pages.
[4] See Appendix A for a list of the many types of fear we harbor.

in building the Kingdom of God. This might include an urge to become more involved in combating one of the evils of our day—abortion, human trafficking, pornography, corruption, the occult. It may be a call to become more involved in the governmental or cultural issues of the day. But you're afraid. You may be reluctant to take a stand for righteousness, fearing what it may cost you.

As we'll see in Joshua's life, there is no quick or simple formula for conquering giants. Rather, we engage in the *process* by living a life of daily obedience to God's precepts.

Whatever your giant is (or are, for there may be several), this study will help you identify them, confront them, engage them in holy warfare, and, through the grace of God, overcome many of them.

Entering the "Promised Land"

Another term used symbolically in this study is "promised land."[5] The Israelites were children of the covenant between God and Abraham. Part of that covenant was the promise of the land inhabited by the Canaanites, a land flowing with milk and honey (see Genesis 13:14-15). When Abraham walked the land, it was sparsely inhabited by various nomadic and semi-nomadic tribes. Now, hundreds of years later, those small nomadic tribes had grown and formed densely populated city-states centered around even larger, fortified cities.

Throughout the history of the Israelites, they knew that God had given them this specific land, even when they did not possess it. Their assignment during the time of Joshua was to finally go in and possess the land the LORD had promised them many generations before. Author and theologian Irving L. Jensen says,

---

[5] For clarity, I refer to the physical geographic land promised to the Israelites as a proper noun using upper case letters (Promised Land), while referring to the symbolic promised land of our journey using lower case letters.

> *The Israelites were promised all the land, but would possess only what they would appropriate and receive from God.*[6]
> ~Irving L. Jensen

How similar this is to our journey.

The land God promised to Abraham centuries before and to Joshua and the Israelites now was enormous. God describes it in Deuteronomy 11:24-25 and reiterates it in Joshua 1:3-4. He says that He is giving them "Every place that the sole of your foot will tread…" In other words, they had to go and take possession of it by physically going there and then fighting for it.

As New Testament believers, we don't have the promise of a specific piece of geography. Nor, contrary to popular belief, do we have promises of happiness, pleasant circumstances, or any of the other temporal pleasures we may desire, although we are assured of peace and even joy amid our struggles.

But we do have the promise that we are being conformed to the image of Jesus Christ.

That is one of our main purposes for living.

That is the work the LORD has promised to do in the life of each believer.

In Romans 8:29, we're told,

> For whom He foreknew, He also *predestined to be conformed to the image of His Son,* … (emphasis added).

---

[6] Irving L. Jensen, *Joshua: Rest-Land Won, Everyman's Bible Commentary* (Chicago, IL: Moody Press, 1966). 36.

2 Corinthians 3:18 further promises,

> But we all, with unveiled face, beholding as in a mirror the glory of the Lord, *are being transformed into the same image* from glory to glory, just as by the Spirit of the Lord (emphasis added).

And 1 John 3:2 assures us,

> Beloved, now we are children of God; and it has not yet been revealed what we shall be, but we know that when He is revealed, *we shall be like Him*, for we shall see Him as He is (emphasis added).

Our human lives are not a struggle for heaven, a place where we believe we will have arrived at spiritual bliss or perfection. Rather, they are an ongoing work of grace, a process often marked by two steps forward and one step backward.

They are lives punctuated by pain, joy, sin, peace, and a wide variety of other emotions and behaviors. Sometimes, we cooperate and experience victory; sometimes, we thwart His work and spend a season wandering in the wilderness.

Yet through it all, in the midst of it all, the Lord *is* working to conform us to the image of His Son.

And that, for the Christian, is our promised land.

It is my prayer that each person who pursues this study will end this time more confident in the power of the Lord your God and better able to stand against the powers and principalities that we are assured *will* assault us as Christians.

Old Testament Warfare | Some Insights

Before we begin the study itself, you'll benefit from understanding the context of the book of Joshua, especially Old Testament warfare and the nature and beliefs of the inhabitants of the Promised Land. Otherwise, especially if you're new to the Old Testament, you're likely to be confused.

The Old Testament's emphasis on warfare seems almost contradictory to the modern mind. We simply do not associate a call to holiness with brutal warfare. In fact, we're often disturbed that the Old Testament details so much destruction carried on in the name of the Lord.

There's no easy answer to this dilemma.

Symbolic

One explanation seems to be that these literal Old Testament battles are symbolic of the all-out struggle between the forces of good and evil in the world. For the child of God, there can be no compromise with evil. Just because things get a little bloody doesn't mean we can expect God to bow out. His purposes are just and good, and He has His sovereign reasons for the means He uses to achieve them. Our task is not to decide what God *ought* to be like but to study what He *is* like as He has revealed Himself to us.

Judgment

Another explanation for the frequency of war in Scripture is that, throughout history, God has used nations to carry out His judgments on evildoers. Occasionally, as with the great flood or the destruction of Sodom and Gomorrah, He judged directly. But more frequently, He used one nation to bring forth His judgment on another when their sin reached some level only God could determine.

Holy War

Holy war, as described in the Old Testament, is not just another war, dressed up by a bit of ritual here and pageantry there. Rather, it follows a distinct pattern that has little in common with ordinary warfare.

Not every case was the same, but a typical example would include many of the following characteristics.

God is the Supreme Commander

First, the LORD Himself was always the Supreme Commander. He usually gave the initial order to fight and was consulted regularly throughout the battle to ensure that the war was in keeping with His will. In fact, often, the battle plan that He required was as illogical and as far from a technically good war strategy as could be imagined. Only a faithful soldier of the LORD could be expected to follow such plans.

Ark of the Covenant

Second, as Supreme Commander, His presence among the warriors was symbolized by the Ark of the Covenant, which always went into battle with them. The number of those in the combat force was not important. The LORD was the real warrior.

Without Him, the largest, strongest, and best-equipped army could not win. With Him, even the smallest army could not lose.

In many accounts, enemy troops broke into confusion and panic even before the battle began.[7] In their blind fear, they often brought about their own destruction. This was no mere coincidence but, rather, was the fantastic result of the presence of the LORD leading the attack. Frequently, the LORD's warriors didn't even get to participate. They simply watched in awe as He confounded the enemy.

A BIT OF HISTORY

God commanded the Israelites to build the Ark of the Covenant at the same time they built the Tabernacle in the wilderness. The Ark was made of acacia wood and was approximately 45 inches long, 27 inches high, and 27 inches deep. It was overlayed with gold inside and out.

On the top was a Mercy Seat, where the Lord promised to meet with His people for atonement of their sins. The Mercy Seat was flanked by two cherubim who faced one another and whose wings touched one another (see Exodus 25). Inside of the Ark they put the stone tablets containing the law, written by the hand of God (see Exodus 25:21), Aaron's rod that budded (see Numbers 17:10), and an omer of manna (see Exodus 16:32-33). These items symbolized the union or covenant between God and His people.

The Ark became the center of worship for generations and was the symbol of divine leadership in battle.

---

[7] For example, see 2 Chronicles 20 and 2 Kings 7:6-8.

Spoils

Another unique characteristic of Old Testament warfare was the disposal of the spoils. Ordinarily, a soldier was allowed to keep any riches he could carry as payment for his services.

In Old Testament warfare, however, the plunder was often "devoted" to the Lord. Sometimes, the soldiers were allowed to keep part of the booty, but often, the spoils belonged to the Lord since He had won the battle.

As we study Joshua's battles, you'll find it helpful to keep these thoughts in mind. As we apply Joshua's lessons to our own lives as New Testament believers, an understanding of Old Testament warfare will enhance those lessons.

The Inhabitants of the Promised Land

The Canaanites

Canaanites was a generic term for all those who lived in the land of Canaan, which was the entire area promised to the then non-existent nation of Israel by the Lord many hundreds of years earlier. In Genesis 15:18-21, the Lord made a covenant with the then-childless Abram, promising,

On the same day the LORD made a covenant with Abram, saying: "To your descendants I have given this land, from the river of Egypt to the great river, the River Euphrates—the Kenites, the Kenezzites, the Kadmonites, the Hittites, the Perizzites, the Rephaim, the Amorites, the Canaanites, the Girgashites, and the Jebusites."

These people were not an organized nation but rather city-states scattered throughout the land. These various tribes were often generically called Canaanites. (You can see the approximate location of the various tribes on the map on page 17)

Pagan Beliefs

The Canaanites, and indeed all the Ancient Near Eastern (ANE) nations, were polytheistic, meaning that they worshipped many gods. This posed a problem for the monotheistic Israelites. The Canaanites were unconcerned at the introduction of a new god into their land—it was just another god. But before long, they convinced many Israelites that the best way to assure their own success was to worship the Lord while at the same time paying homage to the local gods—just in case. Even after 40 years in the wilderness, the Israelites were not thoroughly convinced of the Lord's power.

Baal was the Canaanites' principal god, and Ashtoreth, Baal's wife, was their principal goddess. She personified the reproductive principle in nature—a fertility goddess. She was also known by the Babylonian name of Ishtar and the Greek name of Astarte.

The land was dotted with images of the Baal and Ashtoreth. One of the most predominant of these was the phallic symbol called the Asherah, which was a sacred pole, cone of stone, or even a tree trunk, representing the goddess. The temples of Baal and Ashtoreth were usually located together and were presided over by both male and female temple prostitutes and by hundreds of prophets. The worship of all Canaanite gods was characterized by extravagant orgies. Their temples were centers of debauchery.[8]

---

[8] In later years, the Lord judged every king based on whether he tore down the high places, the locus of this vile pagan worship. Only one king, Josiah, succeeded (see 2 Kings 23:1-25).

Archaeological excavations have provided much insight into the Canaanite religion. For example, excavations at Gezer from 1904 to 1909 found the ruins of a "high place" or temple dedicated to the worship of Baal and Ashtoreth dated just before the Israelite occupation of about 1500 B.C. The structure contained huge quantities of images and plaques of Ashtoreth with rudely exaggerated sex organs designed to foster sensual feelings.

Under the debris in this high place, archaeologists found many jars containing the remains of children who had been sacrificed to Baal. It was common practice for the Canaanites to sacrifice their firstborn children to appease the fertility gods and ensure large families. The whole excavation at Gezer proved to be a cemetery for newborn babies.

The Canaanites worshipped primarily by indulging in fertility rites with temple prostitutes in the presence of their gods as if they were engaging with the gods themselves. They then murdered their firstborn children as a sacrifice to these same gods.

Another common practice was what the Canaanites called "foundation sacrifice." When a house was to be built, a child would be sacrificed, and its body placed in the wall to bring good luck to the rest of the family. Many of these were found in Gezer, Megiddo, Jericho, and other Canaanite cities.

Is it any wonder that God commanded Israel to exterminate the Canaanites? Did a civilization of such abomination and brutality have a right to continue to exist? In fact, many scholars have wondered why God didn't destroy them sooner than He did.

In giving the law to His people, God had warned,

When the LORD your God brings you into the land which you go to possess, and has cast out many nations before you, the Hittites and the Girgashites and the Amorites and the Canaanites and the Perizzites and the Hivites and the Jebusites, seven nations greater and mightier than you, and when the LORD your God delivers them over to you, you shall conquer them *and* utterly destroy them. You shall make no covenant with them nor show mercy to them. Nor shall you make marriages with them. You shall not give your daughter to their son, nor take their daughter for your son. For they will turn your sons away from following Me, to serve other gods; so the anger of the LORD will be aroused against you and destroy you suddenly (Deuteronomy 7:1-4).

God's purpose in the command to exterminate the Canaanites, besides serving as a judgment on them, was to keep Israel from idolatry and depravity. God was preparing Israel for the specific grand purpose of paving the way for the coming of Jesus Christ, the Messiah. To do this, He needed to establish in the world the idea that there is one (and only one) true and living God. If Israel fell into idolatry, then there ceased to be any reason for its existence as a nation. As a matter of precaution, it was essential to cleanse the land of every vestige of idolatrous worship.

> *The wars of Israel were the only 'holy wars' in history, for they were the wars of God against the world of idols.*[9]
> ~*Dietrich Bonhoeffer*

In this regard, Joshua gave Israel a good start. If only Israel had remained faithful to his leadership after his death, what a different story there might have been to tell.

---

[9] D. Bonhoeffer, and E. Metaxas, *The Cost of Discipleship* (Touchstone, 2012), 147.

CANAAN AT THE TIME OF THE CONQUEST

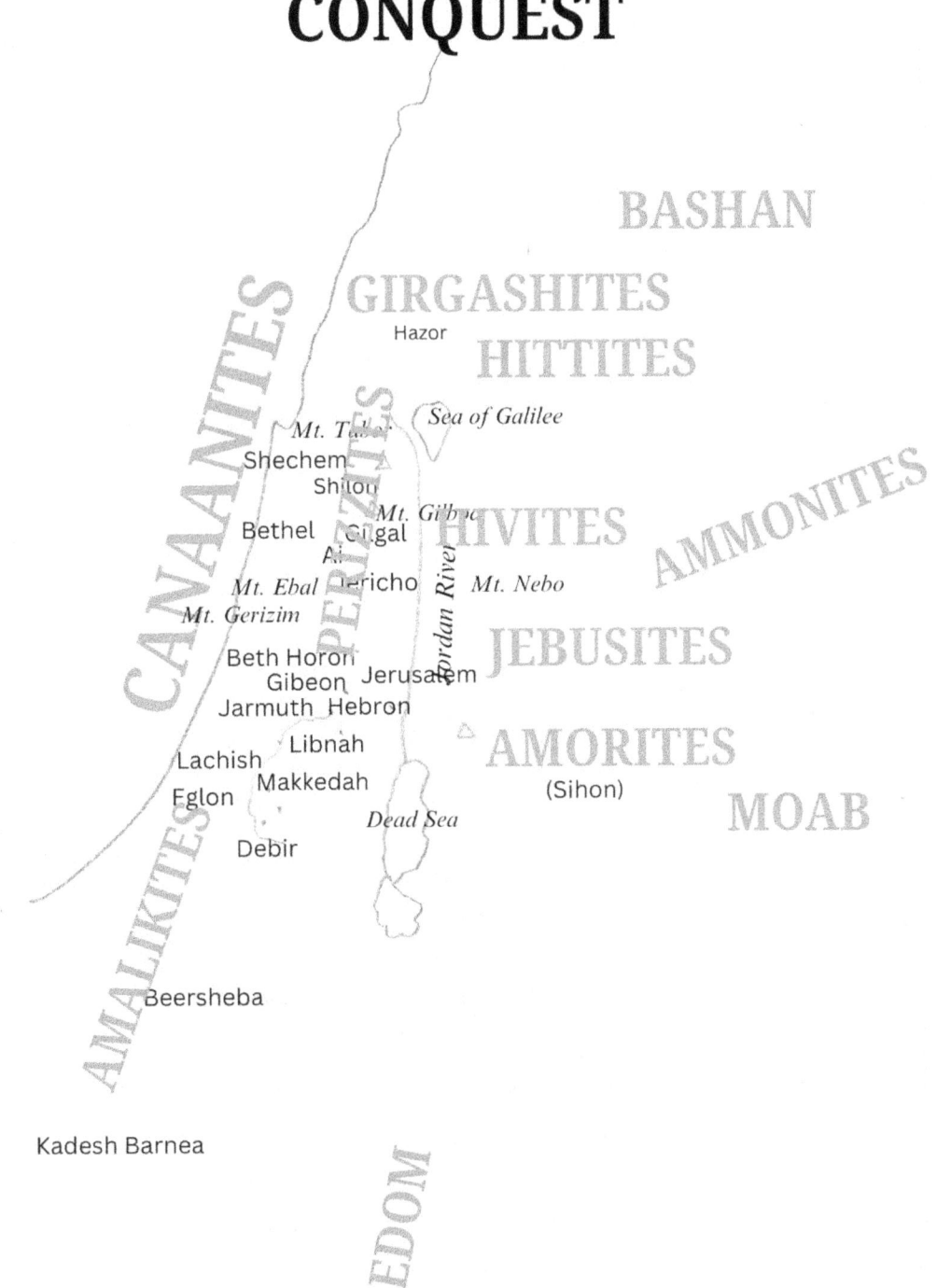

NOTE: The locations of the local tribes are approximate and will not agree with all sources.

TRAINING IN LIFE'S BOOT CAMP

Four years of high school. Four years of college. Another two or three–or more–years of graduate school. Summer jobs. Part-time jobs. Scouting programs. Sunday school. What do all of these—and an endless list of other experiences—have in common? They're all part of our society's attempts to prepare young people for "life," for adulthood.

Yet many experts agree that today, most preparation falls short of providing what people really need to succeed in life. Many kids graduate from school unable to read, do basic math, or use critical thinking skills. Young adults graduate from college and obtain advanced degrees but are overwhelmed by a world where values are relative and ethics are situational. Employees advance by compromising their principles and becoming entangled in the web of "office politics." Executives, more concerned about the bottom line than about crossing the line, sacrifice long-term success on the altar of short-term profits. This is the stuff of which much of our modern society is made.

Given this environment, how can we become people who will succeed with integrity? How can we become people who refuse to compromise for the sake of expediency? Independent thinkers who are capable of standing firm in the face of opposition? Joshua's early years may provide some suggestions.

Getting Started

1. What class, job, or other experience contributed the most to your preparation for the work you do today? Do you consider that it was a positive or a negative preparation?

Most of what I really need to know about how to live and what to do and how to be I learned in Kindergarten. Wisdom was not at the top of the graduate-school mountain, but there in the sandbox at Sunday School.

These are the things I learned:
Share everything.
Play fair.
Don't hit people.
Put things back where you found them.
Clean up your own mess.
Don't take things that aren't yours.
Say you're sorry when you hurt somebody.
Wash your hands before you eat.
Flush.
Warm cookies and cold milk are good for you.
Live a balanced life--learn some and think some
and draw and paint
and sing and dance
and play and work
some every day.[10]

~ Robert Fulghum

---

[10] Robert Fulghum, *All I Really Need to Know I Learned in Kindergarten*, 15th anniversary ed. (New York: Ballantine Books, 2003), 2.

Introducing Joshua

Read Exodus 17:8-16, 24:13-18, 33:7-11; Numbers 11:26-29

We see in these passages that Joshua (who seems to appear out of nowhere) was already an aide to Moses and a leader before he became a military leader.

The battle with the Amalekites was the first of many the nation of Israel would fight in their effort to occupy the Promised Land, the land of the Lord's covenant with their father, Abraham. The Amalekites, descendants of Esau[11] (see Genesis 36:12), lived in the area north of Kadesh.

Why did the Amalekites attack the Israelites? Perhaps they attacked anyone attempting to pass through their land. It's possible they saw the Israelites as vulnerable and wandering people without a homeland or established military. Or there might have been a sense of hostility or a desire to challenge the Israelites as they were gaining strength and recognition following their miraculous deliverance from Egypt.

The Amalekites' attack is portrayed as an unprovoked act of aggression against the Israelites. This conflict is significant in the biblical narrative because it becomes a symbol of enmity. The Lord later told the Israelites to remember the aggression they faced from the Amalekites and commanded His people to blot out their memory from under heaven (see Deuteronomy 25:17-19). Scripture is also clear that these people were idolaters and enemies of the Lord.

As we go along, you will see that the Lord is simultaneously moving His people into the Promised Land and removing idolaters from that land.

---

[11] Esau, brother of Jacob, was the grandfather of Amelek (Genesis 36:12).

2a. How did God begin to prepare Joshua to be a great leader of Israel?

b. What character traits might Joshua have developed through these experiences?

c. How is God preparing you for what lies ahead? What lessons are you learning, or character traits are you developing as you go about your daily activities and responsibilities? (Invest some time in this question and ask a friend or co-worker if necessary. There are more lessons than you are probably aware of, and you might assume they aren't related to where you think you're going. Look again.)

Read Numbers 13 and 14

It took just over two years for the Israelites to travel from Egypt to the border of the Promised Land, including a long stop at Mt. Sinai (see Numbers 10:11). During this time, Joshua faithfully served Moses. Upon reaching the border of Canaan, Moses sent Joshua and eleven other men—one from each tribe—to spy out the land.

Although these spies experienced the richness of the land and acknowledged that it did indeed flow with milk and honey, just as the LORD had promised, they returned after 40 days with a mixed report. Ten spies cried out in fear: "We saw giants there! We seemed like grasshoppers, and we looked the same to them" (Numbers 13:27-33, paraphrased).

God often uses simple, insignificant tests to prepare us to face greater challenges and to shape our character to reflect His glory.

Only Caleb, then about 40 years old, remembered how the LORD had miraculously brought them out of Egypt. He spoke in faith. The community had reached a crisis point, and Joshua was faced with a test of his faith that would determine his destiny. Would he stand with Caleb or the other ten spies? Would he stand with the majority or the minority?

3a. What choice did Joshua make? Why? How do you think he felt? Where was his faith grounded?

b. Describe a time when, like Joshua and Caleb, you stood firm for the LORD in the face of opposition. How did you feel? What was the result?

c. Did your feelings about the situation change or affect what was the right action to take? Why or why not?

d. Do you see things differently in retrospect? If so, what's different?

> *God wasn't asking their opinion. He had already given them the Promised Land. The ten spies thought their opinions mattered. They didn't. Moses sent them to determine how to take the Promised Land, not if they should take it.*

We usually don't know when we're facing a life-changing choice. One that will direct the course of the rest of our life. Such decisions won't be made in the heat of the moment. Rather, they will be based on the character we've *already developed* and the many seemingly small decisions leading up to that moment.

Here's the clincher. God wasn't asking their opinion. He had *already given* them the Promised Land. Somehow, the ten spies thought their opinions mattered. Moses sent them to determine *how* to take the Promised Land, not *if* they should take it.

4a. The Canaanites were an obstacle to the Israelites settling in their Promised Land. Who or what are the giant(s) in your life? What obstacles cause you to fear and threaten to prevent you from reaching your promised land (which we have defined in this study as the process of being conformed to the image of Jesus Christ)?

b. We listed and defined the various types of giants last week. Look back to page 6 to refresh your memory. While you may have many giants in your life, identify ONE that you want to conquer during this study. Be sure to ask God which one He wants you to tackle. It might not be your biggest giant, but rather, one He knows you can conquer in 13 weeks. It also needs to be one you're *willing* to pay the price to conquer. Be honest with yourself and God. Do you *really* want to conquer this one?[12] We'll apply the principles from the book of Joshua to this giant to learn the skill of conquering giants. [Spend some time on this. It's a key question for the rest of the study!]

---

[12] For example, if you're overweight but know in your heart of hearts that you have no interest in or willingness to exercise and change your diet, this is not the giant for you. Choose something you're actually willing to fight for.

> **MY GIANT FOR THIS STUDY IS:**
> **(DESCRIBE IT IN DETAIL)**

5a. Why did the Israelites grumble against the LORD? What emotions do you think they were feeling? What underlying character traits or experiences might have fed these emotions?

b. Do you ever feel these emotions as you face your giant(s)? What is at their root for you? Give an example.

> ## GIANT KILLING STRATEGY
> ## KILL THE "IF ONLY'S"
>
> Often when we think about our giant, we have regrets. We think, "If only I hadn't… " or "If only he or she had…" This immediately binds you to the past and empowers your giant.
>
> The reality is, you can't change the past, so living with "if only's" literally keeps you looking backward instead of forward. The Israelites were still emotionally bound to Egypt, which blinded them to the opportunities ahead of them.
>
> When you encounter an "if only," here's a strategy to disarm it and move ahead.
>
> Change your mindset from "if only" to "I would have liked to (state the behavior your emotions tell you that you want now), but since I didn't, I will now (state the behavior you will, can, or want to do now.)
>
> Example: I would have liked to have handled that situation at work better, but since I didn't, I will carefully evaluate my part in the problem and get whatever help I need to learn the skills to avoid that reaction next time.
>
> This approach releases you from the past and moves you forward into your future.

6a. What was the Israelites' proposed solution to their problem (see Numbers 14:4)?

7a. How did God react to the people's lack of faith? What caused Him to forgive them (see Numbers 14:10-22)?

b. What punishment did He promise for those who rebelled (see Numbers 14:20-35)?

c. How did God reward the faithfulness of Joshua and Caleb (see Numbers 14:24, 30)? Why is this significant?

Choosing not to enter the land was one thing. But now the people were told they *could not* enter the land of promise and, moreover, they were to be punished for 40 years—one year for each day the spies had explored the land. The awful finality of the sentence caused them to grope for a solution, a way to convince God to reconsider.

8a. When the Israelites realized their sin, how did they respond (see Numbers 14:39-45)? What did they do? Why were they guaranteed defeat? (See Exodus 25:22 and Numbers 10:33-36).

b. Describe a time when you were deeply challenged (perhaps by a sermon, speaker, or book) or recognized a deep sin and then overreacted in an attempt to remedy the situation. Was your action motivated by true repentance or by the sin of presumption?

What the Israelites did not realize was that their sin of unbelief affected not only the present generations but also activated a curse that has continued to this day. According to the Mishnah[13] and Rabbinic tradition, this sin of unbelief occurred on the 9th day of the Hebrew month of Av (Tishbi b'Av), which has become a dreaded day in history. For example, the following chart lists just a few of the tragedies that have occurred on the 9th of Av since that fateful day. And yet, the Jews have not repented of this sin and have not turned their faith to Jesus.

---

[13] The Mishnah or the Mishna (מִשְׁנָה,) "study by repetition," is the first written collection of the Jewish oral traditions, also known as the Oral Torah. It is the first work of rabbinic literature, with the oldest surviving material dating to the 6th to 7th centuries BCE.

Hebrew Year	Common Year	Event[14]
2448	(1312)	Spies return from 40 days in Israel with evil reports of the Land of Israel. Jewish people cry in despair, give up hope of entering the Land of Israel.
3340	(421)	Destruction of First Temple by the Babylonians, under Nebuchadnezzar. About 100,000 Jews killed during invasion. Exile of remaining tribes in southern kingdom to Babylon and Persia.
3830	70	Destruction of Second Temple by Romans, under Titus. Over 2,500,000 Jews die as a result of war, famine and disease. Over 1,000,000 Jews exiled to all parts of the Roman Empire. Over 100,000 Jews sold as slaves by Romans. Jews killed and tortured in gladiatorial "games" and pagan celebrations.
3892	132	Bar Kochba revolt crushed. Betar destroyed - over 100,00 killed.
3893	133	Turnus Rufus ploughs site of Temple. Romans build pagan city of Aelia Capitolina on site of Jerusalem.
4855	1095	First Crusade declared by Pope Urban II. 10,000 Jews killed in first month of Crusade. Crusades bring death and destruction to thousands of Jews, totally obliterate many communities in Rhineland and France.
5050	1290	Expulsion of Jews from England, accompanied by pogroms and confiscation of books and property.
5252	1492	Inquisition in Spain and Portugal culminates in the expulsion of the Jews from the Iberian Peninsula. Families separated, many die by drowning, massive loss of property.
5674	1914	Britain and Russia declare war on Germany. First World War begins. First World War issues unresolved, ultimately causing Second World War and Holocaust. 75% of all Jews in war zones. Jews in armies of all sides - 120,000 Jewish casualties in armies. Over 400 pogroms immediately following war in Hungary, Ukraine, Poland and Russia.
5702	1942	Deportations from Warsaw Ghetto to the Treblinka concentration camp begin.
5749	1989	Iraq walks out of talks with Kuwait.
5754	1994	The deadly bombing the building of the AMIA (the Jewish community center in Buenos Aires, Argentina) which killed 86 people and wounded some 300 others.

---

[14] Rabbi Mordechai Becher, "History of Events of Tisha B'av," accessed 2023_12_13, 2023, https://ohr.edu/1088.

> *The wrong of our rebellion and unbelief is not turned to right by attempting the exact opposite. It is still the same spirit which prompted one that influences the other. The obedience which is not of simple faith is self-confidence, and only another kind of unbelief and self-righteousness.*[15]
>
> ~Alfred Edersheim

9a. What was the underlying sin in their actions?

b. What is the difference between faith and presumption?

> *In places of quiet and faithful service, God prepares us to do great things for Him.*

Joshua and Caleb did not participate in the unfruitful attack, an example of their consistency in obeying the LORD even in the face of strong opposition from their peers. However, doubting God's power to lead them, the rest of the nation faltered and lost their opportunity to possess the Promised Land.

Like Israel, many Christians spend years wandering in the wilderness of wasted lives, divided loyalties, or scattered affections. They are not willing to submit to God as the LORD of their lives. Consequently, they fail to appropriate the spiritual blessings available to them in Christ. Some causes of this dilemma are apathy, unbelief, disobedience, and rebellion.

---

[15] Alfred Edersheim, *Old Testament Bible History* (Wilmington, Del: Associated Publishers and Authors), 154.

10. Are there areas of your life where, bound by apathy, unbelief, disobedience, or rebellion, you're living a "grasshopper life?" If so, identify and confess them and identify how they empower your giant. You may need to get help beyond your group if these are deep-seated problems.

Joshua served as Moses' aide for another 38 years[16] as the Israelites wandered in the wilderness before the LORD commissioned him to lead the nation (see Numbers 27:18). Moses was 120 years old when he died (see Deuteronomy 31:2). Joshua was approximately 85 years old when he was appointed as leader of the nation, and he ruled until he was 110.

In God's economy, there is no shortcut to excellence. If I hope to see my life conformed to the image of Jesus Christ, I must be willing to follow His timetable and faithfully fulfill the roles He has chosen for me, even when they seem insignificant. God does not call most of us to be child prodigies. Rather, He simply calls us to a long and faithful obedience as we begin to look more and more like His Son.

MEMORY VERSE: *2 Corinthians 3:18*
But we all, with unveiled face, beholding as in a mirror the glory of the LORD, are being transformed into the same image from glory to glory, just as by the Spirit of the LORD.

---

[16] We typically say the Israelites wandered in the wilderness for 40 years, but God, in his kindness, counted the two years spent at Mt. Sinai as "time served" when he sentenced them to one year for every day the unfaithful spies spent in the land. (See Numbers 14:33-34, Deuteronomy 2:14).

Keys To Conquering My Giant From This Lesson

Consider how you can apply what you've learned in Week 2 as you begin to conquer your giant.

ACTION ITEMS:

A.

B.

C.

Notes & Prayer Requests

WEEK 3
CONQUERING FEAR

Fear! You know the feeling—the churning, almost nauseating knot in your stomach. The constricting adrenaline rush through your throat and out to the tips of your ears. Vision blurred by the sudden whirling of the room. An almost insurmountable urge to flee. And yet, mingled with the fear caused by new, unknown challenges is a twinge of excitement.

What's your tendency when you face a challenge that you know will cause discomfort? Do you eagerly embrace it, mindless of the potential for pain? Do you timidly inch toward it, aware of the risk but also aware of the opportunity? Or do you fearfully spend every ounce of energy determining how to avoid it? How to go around the mountain rather than over it? How to go over the bridge rather than through the raging torrent? Fear can motivate us, or it can immobilize us. The choice is ours.

Joshua was no different from most of us. He had been called to a seemingly impossible task with "only" the assurance of the Lord's presence to instill confidence. And that, as we shall see, was enough for him.

Getting Started

1. Think back to a major "first" in your life—the first day of school or of a new job, for example. What feelings did you experience as you left home that morning? Why?

The only thing we have to fear is fear itself.[17]
~Franklin Delano Roosevelt

Background

After 40 years of wandering in the wilderness, the generation that had sinned against the LORD had died. As the Israelites neared the Promised Land for the second time, they had already defeated two kings and had taken a large territory east of the Jordan.[18]

At their request, Moses had allocated this land to the tribes of Reuben, Gad, and the half-tribe of Manasseh on the condition that their fighting men would cross the Jordan with the rest of Israel and continue to fight until the LORD gave rest to all of them.

---

[17] Franklin Delano Roosevelt, *First Inaugural Address*, March 4, 1933.
[18] Numbers 21:21-35 tells of the defeat of Sihon, king of Heshbon, and Og, the giant king of Bashan, east of the Jordan. These were no small feats. Deuteronomy 2:26-34 tells us they took "all his cities" in defeating Sihon. King Og and his people were the very giants their fathers had feared, but Deuteronomy 3:4 says they took 60 cities. By this time they were well skilled in battle, but entering the Promised Land *still* raised fear in them.

The decision of these two-and-a-half tribes to remain east of the Jordan was not God's will for them. He would have preferred that they enter the heart of the Promised Land rather than settle on its edge. This was a decision they would eventually regret. Their descendants were the first to fall to the Assyrians (see 1 Chronicles 5:25-36).

However, as we face the giants of life, we need to remember that we have the free will to choose how we will walk with God. We can spend years in the wilderness of divided loyalties and lukewarm faith. We can settle down just short of our goal, discouraged by "I can't," "I'm afraid," or "It's too hard!" We can march around the mountain again and again, making the same mistakes. Or, with courage and faith, we can battle our giants, conquer them, and joyfully become transformed into the image of Jesus Christ.

God forbade Moses from entering the Promised Land because of a single act of disobedience (see Numbers 20:1-12). As Moses faced death, the LORD commissioned Joshua to lead the children of the disobedient generation into the Promised Land, the land of giants.

This was no small task. The people of Canaan were stronger and more populous than they had been 40 years earlier. Their cities were more strongly fortified, and their people more sophisticated. By contrast, the Israelites were slightly fewer in number and had little sophistication. They had been nomads for a generation, never settling in one place long enough to develop the culture that was now common to the city dwellers. And yet, the LORD had already given them many victories and much territory east of the Jordan.

As they reached the border of Canaan, Moses ordered a new census to determine how many fighting men were available and how to divide the land and the spoils. With these details out of the way, all that remained was the transfer of power from

Moses to Joshua. The book of Deuteronomy is written in the form of three addresses by Moses to the nation as they camped on the plains of Moab. These addresses review the trip from Egypt, with both its high and low points, and summon the people to faithful obedience to the Lord.[19]

Read Deuteronomy 31:1-29

2a. The Israelites knew they were facing a major change in their lives as Moses spoke to them for the last time. How do you think they felt as they heard this last address from their leader of over 40 years—the only leader most of them had ever known?

b. How do you think Joshua felt as he stood before the congregation to be appointed as their leader? (Remember that as Moses' closest aide for over 40 years, he had experienced firsthand the fickleness of these people.)

---

[19] Deuteronomy is also written in the form of a *suzerain vasal covenant*. See the description of this in "A Bit of History" in Week 9.

> *The true proof of faith consists in this, that when we feel the solicitations of natural fear, we can resist them, and prevent them from attaining an undue ascendancy. Fear and hope may seem opposite and incompatible affections, yet it is proved by observation, that the latter never comes into full sway unless there exists some measure of the former.*[20]
>
> ~John Calvin

3a. What does Moses recognize as the strongest emotion in the people (see Deuteronomy 31:6)? How does he encourage them?

b. What does Moses acknowledge as the strongest emotions in Joshua (see Deuteronomy 31:7-8)? Does Moses have good reason to understand these feelings (see Exodus 3:1-13)? Why? How does he encourage Joshua?

c. What does God recognize in Joshua (see Deuteronomy 31:23)? How does He encourage him?

---

[20] John Calvin, *Commentary on the Book of Psalms*, trans. James Anderson, vol. 2 (1845).

Read Deuteronomy 34:7-8

Even though they knew the transition was coming, the death of their beloved leader wasn't easy. Rather than pushing forward immediately, they stopped and took time to grieve. To weep and mourn. Then, at the end of thirty days, they moved on.

4a. What does verse 8 say happened at the end of thirty days?

b. Is there something related to your giant that needs to die before you can move forward? Describe it. Most likely, it won't be as praiseworthy as Moses. And that's OK.

If you chose your giant well, chances are it's been around for a while. Chances are, you've already tried to conquer it. Probably many times. That's why it's a giant. Each time you fail, it grows stronger and more formidable.

c. Is grief over some aspect of your giant or your life keeping you stuck so you can't move forward? Take some time and ask the LORD if you have unfinished business hindering your successful conquering of your giant. Identify it by name.

d. Decide how much time you will take to mourn this loss. Mourn well, and then move on to your promised land.

NOTE: If your grief and loss seem overwhelming or if you feel unable to move forward, that's an indicator that you need someone to walk through this journey with you. That's what the body of Christ is for. Sometimes, processing with a good friend is enough. Sometimes, your pastor may be able to help. But sometimes, you'll need to work with a trained lay counselor or a professional therapist. They can teach you the skills you need to finally leave the trauma and grief behind. Whatever you do, DON'T stay stuck in trauma and grief, missing your destiny in the process. Get the help you need to move forward. Only then will you be able to conquer your giant.

Read Joshua 1:1-9, Deuteronomy 8:11-18

Joshua had been called to the seemingly impossible task of leading the Israelites into the Promised Land, conquering the giants, and claiming their inheritance. He knew that, in accepting the call, that he would face danger, inconvenience, and criticism.

5a. What else did he know for sure (see Joshua 1:5)?

b. What impossible task or calling do you face? What about this makes it a giant for you?

c. Is this the same giant you identified in Week 2? If not, how is it related?

d. How do you *feel* about this giant? What are the *emotions* you experience?

e. What are the *facts* about this situation? Rewrite verses 2-5, inserting *your* name and details regarding *your* giant(s). Do you believe this?

For as he thinks in his heart, so is he.[21]
~Solomon

One of the greatest "giant-enablers" is confusing the *facts* of a situation with the *feelings* about that situation. In most cases, facts are based on *truth,* while feelings are based on *lies.* It's critical to be able to tell the difference. Feelings, especially those we consider negative, usually loom far bigger and stronger than the facts, seeming to overwhelm us. But when we bring the Truth of God's word to bear on the situation it becomes possible to see things differently and to subdue and eventually conquer even your greatest fear. The fact is, we must not allow our feelings to lead. Feelings and behaviors are based on our beliefs, our mindset. On what we think and believe. Satan, using a spirit of fear, will try to tell us that our catastrophic thoughts are real. But do they agree with Truth and the Word of God? If they don't, they are lies and need to be replaced. This is one form of renewing of the mind.[22] And it's an essential skill in conquering giants.

---

[21] Proverbs 23:7
[22] See 2 Timothy 2:7, Romans 12:1-2, and Ephesians 4:22-25.

GIANT KILLING STRATEGY
DEFEAT LIES BY EMBRACING TRUTH

It is critical that you learn to identify whether what you believe is a lie or the Truth. Lies usually loom large and stoke fear, while Truth is based on or is at least consistent with the Word of God and actual facts. Truth quenches the fear. Here are some examples to help you ferret out the lies and replace them with Truth. Speak Truth over yourself and your giant many times each day.

Lie	Truth
I can't do anything right.	While it may feel I can't do anything right, the Truth is, I have done a lot right in my life and I am fully capable of doing this right if I depend on God. (Phil. 1:6, 4:13)
My life is a total disaster, and I can't beat this problem.	While it may feel as if everything is a mess, God has the resources I need to beat this problem. (2 Cor. 10:4-5)
I don't have enough (time, money, energy, wisdom) to conquer this giant.	While I may feel I don't have enough resources, God says He has already provided everything I need for life and godliness. (2 Peter 1:3)
I'm too afraid to even start. It's too big for me.	While it may feel too big, my God is bigger, and He will be with me every step of the way. (Isaiah 43:2)

6a. What commands and promises did God give to Joshua in verses 2-9? (Note the transition from the general to the specific to the general again.) I've done the first one for you. The shaded spaces indicate no response is needed.

Commands	Promises
v. 2 *Arise, go over this Jordan, you and all this people*	*to the land which I am giving to them—the children of Israel.*
v. 3	
v. 4	
v. 5	
v. 6	
v. 7	
v. 8	
v. 9	

b. What do you think is the key verse in this passage? Why?

c. To whom did Joshua's battle belong? To whom does your battle belong (see 2 Chronicles 20:15-17, Philippians 2:13)?

7a. Did God condemn or criticize Joshua for his fears? Why do you think this is true (see 2 Corinthians 12:9-10)? What did God offer Joshua?

b. How does God respond to your fears?

As we have noted, Joshua was well qualified for the task before him. He had served as aide and confidant of Moses, the friend of God, for over 40 years. He had even accompanied Moses to Mt. Sinai where Moses met with God face-to-face, like a man meets with a friend. Joshua had connections. He had also seen great success in battle and had been personally selected by God to carry on after Moses. A better-qualified man could not be found for this great task.

8a. How did God acknowledge Joshua's outstanding credentials and skills?

b. What credentials and skills do *you* bring to the task of conquering your giant(s)?

c. How useful do you think they will be? (See Deuteronomy 8:11-18, Isaiah 64:6, Philippians 3:3-9.)

9a. What key did God give Joshua to accomplish his goal (v. 8)? Why is this important?

b. Do we have access to this same resource? Explain.

A Bit of History

At the time Joshua takes place in history, about 1400 BC, there were no "books" as we know them. Most history was communicated orally. However, in the perfection of God's timing, a few hundred years before Moses the first rudiments of alphabetic writing were developed. Since Moses was raised in the courts of Egypt, it would make sense that he was among the few who had learned to write.

The Egyptians made paper from the stems of the papyrus, a plant that still grows in the Nile marshlands. From the pounded sheets of papyrus, they made scrolls. This likely is how Moses wrote the laws beyond the 10 Commandments and the other writings we now call Genesis, Exodus, Leviticus, and Numbers. It most likely also contained what we know as the book of Deuteronomy, the actual covenant the LORD made with Israel. This is probably the Book of the Covenant mentioned in Exodus 24:7.

This scroll was not placed in the ark of the covenant, but according to Deuteronomy 31:26, it was placed next to it. By the time of Joshua, he had resources to help him govern.

No one before Joshua had ever been instructed to receive orders from the LORD through the words of writing rather than directly from God Himself. Moses had always received his orders straight from the mouth of God. But now, as Joshua stood at the threshold of the Promised Land, Moses was dead. And while Joshua was still receiving orders directly from God, it appeared that God was asking Joshua to take more responsibility to build his character for his success.

Therefore, Joshua was the first man to learn the Word of God in the same way that we learn: from the written word and through memorization. Joshua was to keep it in his mouth and in his mind. The emphasis for Joshua—and for us—is on making Bible study, memorization, and meditation a constant practice. The result: good success from the hand of God.

> *When our LORD calls us to a seemingly impossible task, He also walks before and beside us until it is completed.*

The sad fact is that we like to take control of our situations so that we can take credit for our success (see Deuteronomy 8:11-18). Or perhaps because we're afraid to trust something as important as our giant to God. (Be honest. Do you *really* think God can handle your giant? Think about that.)

What we need to learn—and often learn the hard way—is that truly successful living is a combination of a promise from God, a gift of God, and attainable only by total reliance on God.

The potential for this type of success is enormous, but so is the risk because just as there are three conditions for success, there are also three enemies of our soul—the world, the flesh, and the devil. Each of these enemies needs to be driven out, just like the giants in the Promised Land. The good news is that they are not only our enemies; they are also enemies of God. And He promises to defeat them *when we fill our thought life and our mouth with the Word of God.*

10a. What are the action steps (v. 8) to being prosperous and successful, to conquering *your* giant?

b. How would you evaluate your obedience in *meditating* on God's Word, day and night, and in *doing* all that is written in it? Why is "meditating" listed before "doing?"

c. How can God's law, His Word, be useful in the battles you face? How can it help you overcome fear? (See Ephesians 6:17, 2 Timothy 3:16-17, Hebrews 4:12).

Through His word, God gives us all the wisdom we need to accomplish what He has called us to do and all the encouragement we need to overcome fear.

Fear is a natural human reaction. In itself, fear is not wrong. In fact, people who feel no fear are considered mentally ill. The key to Christian living, however, is how we handle that fear. When we are sure that GOD is calling us to move forward, to capitulate and refuse to proceed is sin. But when we move forward claiming the promises of God, our faith is increased, and our victory assured.

Conquering fear is the first step to conquering your giant, so "*do it afraid!*"

MEMORY VERSE: *Joshua 1:8*

This Book of the Law shall not depart from your mouth, but you shall meditate in it day and night, that you may observe to do according to all that is written in it. For then you will make your way prosperous, and then you will have good success.

Keys To Conquering My Giant From This Lesson

Consider how you can apply what you've learned in Week 3 as you continue to conquer your giant.

ACTION ITEMS

A.

B.

C.

Notes & Prayer Requests

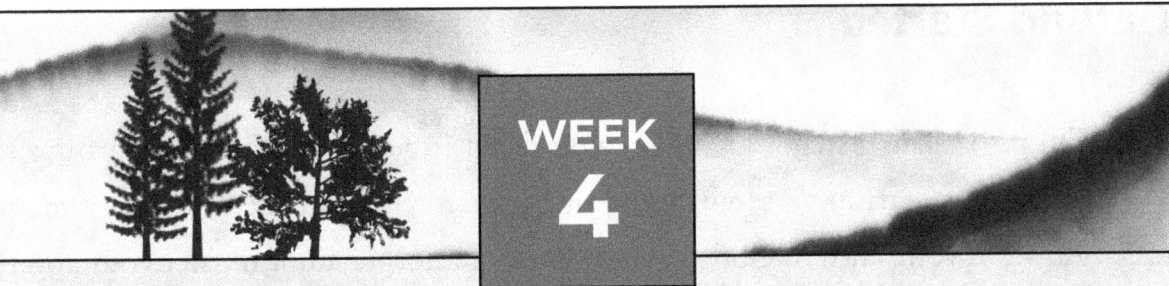

WEEK 4
OVERCOMING OBSTACLES

Obstacles! We all face them. Just when our hopes are the highest, just when we think we're about to accomplish that coveted goal, a new obstacle looms before us. How we respond is a sure measure of our character.

The enemy makes sure we are challenged and, if possible, discouraged by the raging currents of life, particularly when reaching for spiritual goals. The temptation to capitulate, to turn back, is never greater than when circumstances seem to overwhelm us.

What's the difference between the LORD's mighty warrior and the fearful defeatist? Faith! Faith in God's word, His promises, and in His very character. If we're sure that the LORD has called us to defeat the giants in our lives, we can also rest in the FAITH that, even when we don't see the answer, He does.

As the new leader of the Israelites, Joshua had several opportunities to prove that his faith was in the LORD his God, not in the obstacles before him.

Getting Started

1. Think back to a major challenge you faced in your childhood—learning to ride a bike, earning a scouting merit badge, trying out for the varsity team. How did your faith in God, your parents, or another adult muster your ability to accomplish this goal?

Faith is not faith which is not tried.[23]
~Katherine Zell

Read Joshua 1:10-2:1

Faith and hope motivate action. Fear and despair motivate inaction or retreat.

Immediately after he was commissioned and reassured by the LORD, Joshua ordered the people to prepare to cross the Jordan and take possession of their land. He then sent two spies to investigate the territory, especially Jericho. Despite his faith in the LORD, Joshua was not negligent in doing his part. He was careful to follow good military form and send in spies before committing his whole army to the conquest of Jericho. This was not a lack of faith on his part, but simply wise stewardship. Once again, the mission of the spies was not to determine *if* they should attack but rather *how* and *when*.

---
[23] Katherine Zell (1497 -- 1562), Den Leydenden Christglaubigen (1524), (To Suffering Believers in Christ).

2. Is there some small but prudent action you need to take in preparation for conquering your giant—your own "spying out the land"? Something that will provide you with much-needed information, faith, and/or confidence? What is it? Why do you think this step is important?

Read Joshua 2:2-24

Divine Providence directed the spies to the house of Rahab, a prostitute, who took them in and hid them from the king of Jericho. Rahab was a perfect accomplice for the spies since it would not arouse suspicion for two strangers to seek her out. Because of her profession, she no doubt had heard the tales of this strange band of nomads that had left Egypt so miraculously, had wandered in the desert for almost 40 years, and had only recently won great victories against the Sihon, king of the Amorites, and Og, king of Bashan. Surely, the Lord had already begun to translate this information from her head to her heart and finally to her will as she believed in Him as the only true God. She was prepared for her guests.

3a. What did the spies learn from Rahab about what the Canaanites thought of the Israelites?

b. Read Exodus 15:14-19. How did Rahab's act of faith fulfill the prophecy of Moses in that passage?

c. What had Rahab come to believe about their God? Upon what did she base this faith?

d. Based on this faith, what did she request?

4. Because of her faith and her active obedience, what eventually happened to this woman? (See Matthew 1:5).

5a. When the spies returned to Joshua, what did they report? How did this differ from the report of the spies 38 years earlier?[24]

---

[24] There may be some confusion regarding this timing. God graciously included the two years they spent at Mount Sinai receiving the Torah and forming the structure for their society in the total 40-year period of punishment. The Israelites crossed the Jordan on the tenth day of the first month, five days short of 40 years after coming out of Egypt and 40 years to the day of the first Passover (see Joshua 4:19).

b. Had the *circumstances* of their conquest changed from 38 years ago? What had changed?

> *Trust in God's help for Christlike living does not preclude being forewarned of the tactics of Satan and being alert to this one who goes about seeking whom he may devour, as he works through such destroyers as lust, pride, disobedience, doubt, discouragement, and neglect.* [25]
>
> ~Irving L. Jensen

Read Joshua 3

Immediately upon receiving the good report from the spies, Joshua and all the Israelites moved to the east bank of the Jordan and camped there. Although they did not know God's next step for them, they moved out in faith to what they *did* know—the Jordan had to be crossed to enter the Promised Land. Since leaving Egypt forty years earlier, they had not had to take any initiative to reach to Promised Land. They simply followed the pillar of cloud by day and the fire by night (see Exodus 13:21). When it moved, they moved. When it rested, they rested.

Now, they had to take the initiative to drive out the idolatrous nations. They were suddenly on the offensive while the Canaanites waited in dread for their sure conquerors.

---

[25] Jensen, 40.

From a purely strategic perspective, the task was impossible. A tributary flowing into the Jordan River at this spot deposited enough silt to create a shallow ford where the water was typically three to four feet deep. But the Jordan was at flood stage, which meant the river could be 10 to 12 feet deep and 140 feet across,[26] making it impassable even for strong young men.

How could Joshua get two million men, women, and children, plus their possessions, across this raging river? And it had to be done in one day. They couldn't leave half the people on either side. From a human perspective, this was an impossible challenge. Joshua could do no more than wait on God for direction.

> *When we know either the direction the Lord wants us to move or the destination He wants us to reach, we are responsible for obediently moving forward in faith, trusting Him to either open the next door or change our direction.*

After three days, the Israelites set out to cross the Jordan. Apparently, God had given Joshua his next set of instructions. The priests were ordered to carry the Ark of the Covenant,[27] 1,000 yards ahead of the tribes. This was the visible sign of divine leadership and the Presence of God.

6a. How are you moving in the direction the LORD wants you to, even though you don't see the whole plan ahead? How are you stepping out in faith *toward* your goal, not knowing specifically *how* the LORD will overcome the next barrier?

---

[26] John A. Beck, "The Narrative-Geographical Shaping of Joshua 3-4," JETS 48/4 (Dec. 2005) 694-96, quoted in Boyd Seevers, *Warfare in the Old Testament: The Organization, Weapons, and Tactics of Ancient near Eastern Armies* (Kregel Academic, 2013), 41.

[27] See page 29 if you aren't familiar with the Ark of the Covenant.

CONQUERING YOUR GIANTS

b. What is that next step for you?

7a. What instructions did the officers of the camp give the people as they ordered them to cross the Jordan behind the Ark of the Covenant? What was the purpose of the Ark?

b. We no longer have the Ark of the Covenant to lead us, and we no longer need to walk 1,000 yards behind the presence of God as we follow His lead. What has He given us instead to guide us since we "have never been this way before?" (See John 14:16-18, 26; 16:13).

Ordinarily, the inhabitants of Jericho would not have been concerned about this army across the river. After all, the Jordan was at flood stage. No army—and certainly no army with such a throng of civilians, animals, and possessions—could cross such a river. But perhaps this time was different, for Jericho had heard how the LORD had pushed back the water of the Red Sea for the Israelites.

And indeed, this time was different, for as the Ark of the Covenant led the way into the Jordan, the waters piled up in a heap. Surely for this generation of Israelites, this miracle was as astonishing and impressive as the parting of the Red Sea had been for their fathers. They had heard the story of the Red Sea many times—some even remembered it from their childhood. And now they were experiencing something equally incredible!

> *...the bigger the obstacle the greater the manifestation of God's might. God requires faith in the face of the obstacle, but he will always go before.* [28]
>
> ~Irving L. Jensen

8a. Do you think it took any more of the LORD's power to divide the Jordan at flood stage than it would have for Him to divide it at trickle stage? Why do you think His plan called for them to cross at flood stage?

b. Does it take any more of God's power for Him to conquer your giant than for Him to deal with the minor, daily problems in your life? Why do you think you are faced with this giant? (See Mark 2:1-12).

c. Where was Joshua's focus when he instructed the priests to step into the flood? Where is your focus as you face your giant?

---

[28] Jensen, 48.

For all of us, there are bound to be formidable 'floods' in the stream of life. Just as Joshua...now faced a raging river that overflowed its banks and inundated the flood plain, so will we. God does not try to hold us back from the rampaging currents of life. He does not ask us to retreat or withdraw from that threat which would seem to engulf us. He does not urge us to try and find some way around the apparently impossible barriers before us. Rather He asks us to believe quietly that:

It is He who brought us here.
It is He who will keep and preserve us here.
It is He who will take us on from here.

For ultimately it is the LORD who shows Himself strong on behalf of those who will without fear or foreboding quietly step out into the surging streams of life. There they will see what great wonders God can perform. They never happen if we hold back on the riverbank waiting for the dry weather season to come [29]
~W. Phillip Keller

Read Joshua 4

The Israelites—two million men, women, and children, with their livestock and possessions—crossed the Jordan on dry land. Imagine how they must have felt as they crossed, knowing that as soon as they reached the other side, the waters would resume their raging flow. Knowing that they were irrevocably committed to conquering the giants of the Promised Land. Knowing there could be no turning back. The LORD had not promised to part the waters again for their retreat.

---
[29] Keller, 73.

> ## GIANT KILLING STRATEGY
> ## BURN THE BOATS!
>
> Upon arriving in Mexico in 1519, Spanish invader Hernán Cortés ordered his men to burn their boats, making it clear that there was no turning back. He wanted to motivate his soldiers to conquer the land or die trying without any hope of escape.
>
> Before we get serious about conquering our giants, we tend to leave a loophole. A way out. A way back. Hedge our bets. Plan B. Just in case. But if we're serious about conquering our giant, we may need to burn the boats.

9. Is there a step of faith you need to take to "burn your boat? A step that will irrevocably commit you to move forward to conquer your giant(s)? What is it? What is keeping you from taking this step?

When all had crossed safely, Joshua commanded them to select twelve stones to set up as a memorial and a sign among them. This was not a mere ritual but a magnificent act of praise and gratitude to God. The stones were symbolic not only of God's faithfulness but also of the people's bold obedience.

10. What have you done or set aside as a memorial to God's work in your life? This might be something as simple as a memorial stone or a journal entry. It might be a picture or poster for your wall. What reminds you of God's faithfulness to date? Why is this important?

The Israelites crossed the Jordan on the tenth day of the first month, five days short of 40 years after coming out of Egypt and 40 years to the day of the first Passover. This was, according to commentator Matthew Henry,[30] a symbol of how little pleasure God takes in punishing His people and how swift He is to show mercy. As a symbol of His covenant with them, He allowed them to celebrate the Passover *in* the Promised Land.

Read Joshua 5

While the military leaders may have favored an immediate offensive, taking advantage of the element of surprise, this was not to be God's way. He is never in a hurry, although His children often are. Two essential rites needed to be re-instituted for the Israelites to be fully restored to their covenant relationship with the Lord: circumcision and the celebration of the Passover. These took place at Gilgal, just a few miles from Jericho, right in the presence of their enemies (see Psalm 23:5).

---

[30] Leslie F. Church, F.R.Hist.S, ed., *Commentary on the Whole Bible by Matthew Henry*, 1 vols. (Grand Rapids, Mich: Zondervan Publishing House, 1961), 216.

Circumcision was the sign of the Lord's covenant with Abraham and his descendants (see Genesis 17:11). However, this rite had been suspended during the forty years the nation wandered in the wilderness because of Israel's sin. Since the judgment was a national one, everyone, including young people and babies born in the wilderness, had to live as a punished nation. Until that sentence was lifted, the rite of circumcision was purposeless and so was discontinued.[31] As they entered the Promised Land, they were invited to renew the covenant by circumcising all the men and boys born in the past forty years.

The nation exercised tremendous faith in performing circumcision since this rendered their fighting men helpless for several days and made them most vulnerable to attack.

Israel's first Passover had been observed in Egypt some 40 years earlier (see Exodus 12: 1-20). Then, the slaying of the paschal lamb and the application of the blood to the doorposts and lintels anticipated deliverance from the oppression of that land and slavery. The blood was a token assuring their deliverance. Israel's second Passover had been observed in the wilderness when the expectation of reaching the Promised Land was high before the spies had been sent out (see Numbers 9:5).

Now, as the new generation reached Canaan and slayed the Passover lamb, they recalled how God had delivered their forefathers out of Egypt, and they anticipated the Lord's faithfulness in the battles to come. This Passover sacrifice stirred up fresh hopes of deliverance.

After they celebrated the Passover, eating of the fruits of the land, the manna stopped. The manna had symbolized (1) their wilderness state and (2) an extraordinary provision they no longer needed.

---

[31] Jensen, 49.

11a. Is there a rite, habit, or action that you need to re-establish (or establish) to be more fully restored to your covenant relationship with the Lord?

b. Is there "manna" in your life that you no longer need, symbolizing an immature relationship with God? Can you give Him permission to remove it and to make you responsible for feeding yourself from the food of your promised land? What does this involve for you?

12a. In the past, the Lord had spoken to Joshua. Now, when Joshua needed even greater encouragement, he experienced the glory of the Lord. How did this great leader respond? What did his response indicate?

b. As you have faced your giant(s) in the past few lessons, how have you experienced the glory of the Lord in a way that is different from your normal experience? How did you respond?

Joshua then meets the Commander of the Lord's army and quickly receives a change of perspective. This was not to be the usual battle between human armies in search of divine favor. Rather, it was a *divine* battle in which human armies would participate. And that's really the perspective of the Kingdom. We can talk about God being on our side; Scripture certainly does (Psalm 56:9, 118:6; Romans 8:31; Hebrews 13:6). But in truth, He doesn't fight our battles simply because we ask him to. He fights our battles because they are actually His battles... He is not our mascot; He's our commander. There's a difference.[32]

> *[Joshua] was anticipating a battle between the Israelite and Canaanite armies. He had thought this was to be his war, until he confronted the divine Commander and learned that the battle was the Lord's. The Captain of the Lord's host had not come to be an idle spectator of the conflict; neither was He an ally. Rather, He was in complete charge and would shortly reveal His plans for the capture of the citadel of Jericho.*[33]
> ~Donald K. Campbell

If Joshua had stopped to analyze every obstacle he would face in reaching the Promised Land, he might never have crossed the Jordan River. The LORD had not given him the complete strategy for conquering the giants of the land but rather had given him only one step at a time. Joshua was required to press forward with little more than his faith in God. And that, it seems, was enough.

MEMORY VERSE: *2 Corinthians 5:7*
For we walk by faith, not by sight.

---

[32] Chris Tiegreen, *Heaven on Earth* (Tyndale, 2015), 204. Paraphrased.
[33] Donald K. Campbell, *Joshua, Leader under Fire* (Wheaton, IL: Victor Books, 1986), 47.

Keys To Conquering My Giant From This Lesson

Consider how you can apply what you've learned in Week 4 as you continue to conquer your giant.

ACTION ITEMS

A.

B.

C.

Notes & Prayer Requests

WEEK 5
DEMOLISHING STRONGHOLDS[34]

"Just when I finally figure out where it's at, somebody moves it!"[35] Joshua must have known that feeling as he realized the LORD's plan for conquering Jericho. It certainly wasn't at all like he might have planned or expected!

Paradox is the norm for the Christian. As believers, we learn to expect the unexpected in our walk with the LORD. Just when we think we know how He will work, He surprises us. Yet the greatest surprise of all is how *well* His plans work—and how so often, ours clearly would have failed.

---

[34] A stronghold in military terms is a building or position that is strongly defended, like Jericho. A stronghold for an individual may be a thought, mindset, or emotion that creates what seems like an insurmountable obstacle to healing or conquering a giant.

[35] Ziggy cartoon, date and source unknown.

Getting Started

1. What are you best or most expert at doing? How do you use this skill, talent, or trait in serving the LORD?

A real Christian is an odd number, anyway.
He feels supreme love
for One whom he has never seen;
talks familiarly every day to Someone he cannot see;
expects to go to heaven on the virtue of Another;
empties himself in order to be full;
admits he is wrong so he can be declared right;
goes down in order to get up;
is strongest when he is weakest;
richest when he is poorest and happiest when he feels the worst.
He dies so he can live;
forsakes in order to have;
gives away so he can keep;
sees the invisible;
hears the inaudible;
and knows that which passeth knowledge. [36]
~A.W. Tozer

---

[36] A.W. Tozer, *The Root of the Righteous* (Harrisburg, PA: Christian Publications, 1955), 156.

Background

Although Jericho was clearly a stronghold, there are at least three reasons why the LORD had Israel enter Palestine there:

1. Jericho was the gateway city that controlled the movements of people to and from central Palestine. Any desert tribe that had ambitions of conquest in the central hill country must first reckon with Jericho. There could be no meaningful infiltration of Canaan from the east without first crushing the gateway city. Jericho must be conquered, or the campaign would fail.[37]

2. An attack from the east would meet the least resistance. The great world powers of the day, such as Egypt and Mesopotamia, had vital interests in the commercial trade route that ran along the western coast of Palestine. Had the attack come from the south or southwest, this trade route would have been threatened and Israel would have found itself involved in a conflict of international dimensions. But skirmishes at Jericho would arouse no interest in either Egypt or Mesopotamia. Israel could obtain a solid foothold on the mainland without arousing international suspicions.[38]

3. The camp at Gilgal, six miles away, had many water reserves, providing a good base camp for the families of the warriors.

---

[37] Harley Swiggum, *The Bethel Bible Series: Old Testament* (Madison, Wisconsin: The Adult Christian Education Foundation, 1961, 1981), 69.
[38] Swiggum, 69.

 **A BIT OF HISTORY**

Archaeological excavations have shown that the outer city wall of Jericho was 32 feet high, from four inches to two feet thick, and made of sun-dried bricks. An inner wall was 11 to 12 feet thick and constructed on the foundation of an earlier wall. The space between the two was from 12 to 27 feet. At frequent intervals, the two were tied together by additional brick walls. This was a formidable barrier for the Israelites to face; it had always offered the inhabitants of Jericho almost unquestioned protection. Excavations confirm charred remains and fallen walls throughout the seven acres of the city.

Read Joshua 6

2. Describe the "walls" encircling and protecting your giant(s). What have you done in the past to try to go over or get through or tear down these walls?

The strongest and highest walls cannot hold out against Omnipotence.[39]

~Matthew Henry

---

[39] Church, 218.

As Joshua faced Jericho, he received instructions for his next step. The LORD not only told him what to do, but what the outcome *already was*. The sense or aspect of the Hebrew verb for "have given" is a "perfect of certitude, indicating the certainty of the action."[40] It describes a future action as if it were already accomplished. Joshua was asked to "walk by faith, not by sight" (2 Corinthians 5:7).

The paradox is that Joshua, the trained and excellent military leader, was asked to use a non-military tactic for the first seven days. He was not allowed to simply take Jericho by force but rather was given a tactic to weaken the resolve of the enemy while building the faith of the Israelites. However, unlike Moses, who had argued eloquently against God's plan to free the Israelites from Pharaoh's grip, Joshua seems to have responded with unquestioning obedience.

> *It appears that the Israelites were given orders on a daily basis, so that their obedience was not a once-for-all matter, but a new challenge every morning. That is the way God generally deals with us too. We live today with little or no knowledge of tomorrow.*[41]
>
> ~Donald K. Campbell

3a. If you were Joshua, the great military leader, how might you have responded to God's plan? How did Joshua respond? What helped him to respond as he did?

---

[40] ———, *The NET Bible Second Edition Notes (NET Notes)*, Second Edition Notes (NET Notes) ed. (Nashville, TN: Thomas Nelson, 2019), 5.8, OakTree Software, Inc.
[41] Campbell, 52.

b. If you were one of the usually stiff-necked Israelites, how might you have responded to this plan? How did the people respond? What does this tell you about their faith?

Faith expressed in obedience to God's Word is always the key to victory.[42]

~Donald K. Campbell

For six hot, blistering days, Israel marched around Jericho. This demanded sustained discipline. It demanded consistent submission to Joshua as their leader. It took time and endurance for no apparent reason. They were not to grumble or break rank or take a break. And all the while, nothing seemed to happen. And then, on the seventh day, instead of marching around the sunbaked walls once for an hour or so, they marched around it seven times, probably without food or water. This day-long ordeal of over 20 miles would have consumed most of the day. The troops would have been at the point of exhaustion.

No one knew whether the enemy's jeers came more from confidence in their defenses or from fear because of the reputation of the attackers, both of which were substantial. Taunts were a typical part of the game, except that the order had come down that the Israelites were not to return them here at Jericho.[43]

~Boyd Seevers

---

[42] Campbell, 51.
[43] Seevers, 32.

c. Describe how you think the Israelites[44] felt after several days of marching around the city, possibly enduring the insults and ridicule of the inhabitants of Jericho and feeling as if they were wasting their valuable time. Do you think some might have been tempted to either retreat or resort to their own "more logical" tactics?

d. Who or what taunts you as you attempt to break down your giant's walls? How should you respond? Are you often frustrated by the lack of instant results?

e. Read Matthew 4:1-11. How was Jesus taunted? How did He respond each time? How does the way He responded inform how you might respond?

4a. Use a dictionary to define the word "paradox."

---

[44] Although the Hebrew uses the word for people, it is most likely that only the "men able to go to war" (see Numbers 26:3) participated in this ritual. But there were 601,730 of them! (See Numbers 26:51).

b. God may also be calling us to use tactics that differ from the obvious. Read at least four of the following passages. How, if at all, do those paradoxical commands relate to how you must face your giant(s)? I've done the first one for you.

Passage	Paradox	Tool to Face Your Giant
Matthew 5:43-44	*Love your enemies, bless those who curse you, do good to those who hate you, and pray for those who spitefully use you and persecute you,*	*Come in the opposite spirit and catch them off guard.*
Matthew 6:25-34		
Matthew 16:24-25		
Matthew 18:3-4		
Matthew 19:21, 23-24		

Passage	Paradox	Tool to Face Your Giant
Matthew 20: 25-27		
1 Corinthians 3:19		
2 Corinthians 12:9-10		
Philippians 2:3		
James 1:2		

c. What paradoxical command is the Lord calling you to use to break down your walls or those that relate more directly to your giant(s)? Cite specific verses and discuss them.

d. Is what God is telling you to do to tackle your giant any more unlikely or ridiculous than what the Israelites were asked to do at Jericho? Explain.

e. Are you willing to obey these paradoxical instructions? Why or why not? Can you ask for prayer and support in obeying?

f. What are the weapons of our warfare? (See 2 Corinthians 10:4-5). Who has primary responsibility here?

GIANT KILLING STRATEGY
DO THE OPPOSITE

You've been attacking your giant in the same way for—well, forever. How's that working out for you? We see in Scripture that the way of the Kingdom is upside down and inside out from the way of the world.

What if, just for fun, you tried responding in the opposite spirit? If you usually swear and yell, try speaking softly. If you usually scowl, try smiling. If you're usually vengeful, try forgiving. I know. It sounds impossible. But that's how God created us to live as Kingdom carriers. To bring heaven to earth (see Matthew 6:10). You'll be amazed at the results.

The Institute of Heart Math has done several studies showing that the energy from your heart can be measured some distance from your body. That energy changes the electromagnetic atmosphere where you are. If you are happy and thinking pleasant thoughts, it changes the atmosphere around you for good. Likewise, if you're upset and angry, the atmosphere around you becomes negative and affects anyone nearby.[45] Don't believe me? Try it in a long, slow post office or grocery store line.

---

[45] One such study is Rollin Ph.D. McCraty, Mike Atkinson, Dana Tomasino, B.A., and William A. Tiller, Ph.D., "The Electricity of Touch: Detection and Measurement of Cardiac Energy Exchange between People," 1998.

Jericho was the first of many strongholds the Israelites would face. It was conquered solely in God's way and with His help to inspire confidence as the nation began its conquest of these powerful people. It is possible, even probable, that what you see as your giant is only your Jericho, the gateway to even greater accomplishments. As you conquer this giant, you, too, will gain the confidence to conquer even greater giants for Him.

> *When we do God's task God's way, the marvelous victory inspires confidence for the next battle we face.*

MEMORY VERSE: *2 Corinthians 10:4-5*
*The weapons **we** fight with are not the weapons of the world. On the contrary, they have divine power to demolish strongholds. **We** demolish arguments and every pretension that sets itself up against the knowledge of God, and **we** take captive every thought to make it obedient to Christ.*

Keys To Conquering My Giant From This Lesson

Consider how you can apply what you've learned in Week 5 as you continue to conquer your giant.

ACTION ITEMS

A.

B.

C.

Notes & Prayer Requests

WEEK 6
LEARNING TO WAIT

Delayed gratification. That's a high-sounding phrase for the need to wait for something you really want. It often carries the prospect of greater rewards for the waiting. Throughout life, we experience this phenomenon. As children, we're told to wait for dinner, wait for a snack, wait to go to the park, wait, wait, wait … Graduation from high school brings another choice. Do we go out into the world immediately—or do we go to college, delaying the opportunity to earn money now for the promise of more later? Career, marriage, parenthood… It seems that almost every fork in our road involves some form of delayed gratification.

The Israelites faced the same choice. Having conquered Jericho, they were told to devote *all* the spoils of the city to the LORD. This was unusual in the warfare of that day. Warriors were usually paid by taking all the plunder they could carry. But in this battle, their first in the Promised Land, they were told to take *nothing* for themselves. They also faced the prospect of years of warfare before they could truly take possession of the land the LORD had given them. Would it be worth it?

Getting Started

1. Describe a delayed gratification choice you made in your youth. Why did you make that choice? Was it worth it?

Everything comes if a man will only wait.[46]
~ Benjamin Disraeli

Background

The city of Jericho was unique not only in its method of conquest but also in its required disposition. Joshua 6:17 tells us, "Now the city shall be doomed by the Lord to destruction, it and all who are in it." The Hebrew word for "doomed to destruction" is *herem* or *cherem*, which means something that was irrevocably given over to the Lord and could no longer be used for secular purposes. This was usually accomplished by burning or otherwise totally destroying the item, although gold, silver, bronze, or iron items often were totally devoted to use in the temple or in the service of the Lord.

Only Jericho was totally destroyed like this. In most future conquests, only the people would be destroyed, while the Israelites were free to take and enjoy the cities, livestock, riches, and stores of the conquered people. Alfred Edersheim suggests,

---

[46] Benjamin Disraeli, <u>Tancred</u>, book IV, ch. 8.

> ... it was fitting that Jericho should have been entirely devoted unto the Lord; not only that Israel might gain no immediate spoil by what the Lord had done, but also because the city, as the firstfruits of the conquest of the land, belonged to Jehovah, just as all the first, both in His people and in all that was theirs, was HIS—in token that the whole was really God's property, Who gave everything to His people and at whose hands they held their possessions.[47]

The word firstfruits was introduced in Exodus 23:16-19 as if it were a known practice. Indeed, we see Cain and Able making offerings to the Lord in Genesis 4. We aren't told what, if anything, the Lord told Adam and Eve and their descendants about how to make offerings to Him, but the practice seems to go back to them. The word firstfruits is used 24 times in the Old Testament, mostly in Exodus and Leviticus. The idea is simply to bring the first of your harvest, your income, or your gain and offer it to the Lord. In the Old Testament, these items were often burned as a fragrant offering to acknowledge the Lord for his provision.

Today we aren't called to totally destroy people or usually even things. Yet even today, the concept of devoting to the Lord is essential to the conquering of our giants.

Read Joshua 6:17-27

2a. What was to be devoted to the Lord? What happened to the devoted things? Was there any exception to this? If so, why?

---

[47] Edersheim, 192-3.

b. What did God warn would be the penalty if anyone took a devoted thing?

We need to briefly digress from the book of Joshua to understand the reasons for these seemingly strange orders.

Read Deuteronomy 7

Idolatry was an issue that would haunt ancient Israel for its entire life. As discussed in Week 1, the people of the land were polytheists. That is, they worshipped more than one god. This was a problem for the Lord, who wanted an exclusive relationship with His people. He considered worshiping other gods the equivalent of adultery.

Totally destroy idols that give you strife so the love of God can direct your life.

3a. Why was the Lord so insistent that the Israelites totally destroy the people? Why not make a treaty with them? (See also Deuteronomy 20:16-18).

b. What was to be done with their idols? Why was the Lord so insistent on this?

c. What idols in *your* life need to be *totally destroyed*? Why? How do they affect your relationship with God?

d. What giants or idols in your life need to be *totally devoted* to the Lord? (Today "devoting" is more often an attitude of the heart rather than physically putting these things in the Lord's temple.) What, because of your attitude toward it, has become a snare to you? Describe the "snare."

4a. What does God promise as the blessings for obedience in these areas?

b. Are there giants in your life that you know should be totally destroyed or devoted, but which you have only "put in the closet," hoping they would go away on their own? Or thinking you might want to pull them out later? Perhaps this is an attitude, behavior, or habit that you have set aside (or tried to set aside) but have not yet totally devoted to the Lord. What are these?

5a. Why did the LORD choose the Israelites to receive His covenant? Why did He keep His covenant and bring them out of slavery in Egypt? How much of this had to do with their personal or corporate qualities?

b. Why has He chosen you? (See John 3:16, 1 John 4:10, Romans 5:8).

c. Who does God say you are? What has He brought you out of? What has He called you into? (See 1 Peter 2:9).

d. How will you respond to this knowledge? Ask for prayer or help if needed.

6a. As we face the prospect of totally destroying some giants and totally devoting others, fear (even panic) may once again grip us. How did the LORD anticipate this fear in the Israelites (see Deuteronomy 7:17-24)? His reminder has three elements. What are they?

> *When all else fails we must be willing to* **Do It Afraid!**

1	
2	
3	

b. How else does He reassure us of victory and freedom from fear?

- 2 Timothy 1:7

- I John 4:18

7a. Rather than one massive victory, how did the LORD promise He would drive the giants from the land? Why? (See Deuteronomy 7:22).

b. We don't expect to be overcome by wild animals today. Why would the Lord still work in us "little by little"?

It is undoubtedly impossible to cut away everything at once from hard hearts, since one who strives to ascend to the highest place must needs rise by steps or paces, and not by leaps.[48]

~Gregory the Great

Read Ephesians 4:20-24

The Greek words for "putting off" and "putting on" suggest changing your clothes, taking off dirty clothes, and putting on something new and fresh. It's helpful to use that mental image as you replace the old with the new regarding your giant. This might be an attitude, like putting off fear and putting on boldness. Or it might be a behavior, like putting off sugar and putting on fruits and vegetables. The key is to do both. Don't run around naked!

8a. What do you need to "put off" regarding your giant? What do you need to "put on" instead? Think about *how* you might do this. What tools, strategies, or help do you need? The reality is, if you could have done this yourself, you would have. What specific changes need to be made to conquer your giant? List them in the table below.

---

[48] Gregory the Great, *Epistle Lxxvi.: To Mellitus, Abbot*, Vol XIII, p 84.

PUT OFF	PUT ON	TOOLS, STRATEGIES, HELP

b. Are you sometimes discouraged or angry with God because He doesn't work faster? If so, confess these emotions and decide to see His hand in the "little by little" victories he gives you.

GIANT KILLING STRATEGIES
NAILING IT TO THE CROSS

We have a resource Joshua and the Israelites didn't have. We have the cross and the blood of Jesus. When we discover or are confronted by a giant or the symptoms (buddies) of that giant, we are invited to simply take them to the cross. Here's a simple five-step strategy I use frequently.

1. Identify a sin, an idol, a behavior, an attitude—anything that is empowering your giant or holding it in place. Let's say it's anger and that anger results in feeling sorry for yourself.

2. In your mind, pick up or gather up all the anger and self-pity and visualize nailing it to the cross. Bang! Bang! Bang! Let the blood of Jesus cover them.

3. Repent for allowing that anger and self-pity to have any part of your body, soul, or spirit. Verbally break the agreement you've had with them and renounce the idolatry involved in that association. (You wanted those behaviors and feelings more than you wanted God).

4. Imagine yourself turning and walking away from those things. Decide to leave them at the cross for Jesus to deal with.

5. Turn to the Father and receive His embrace and forgiveness. Listen to receive what he has for you in exchange. He will always give us good (something to "put on") when we release (put off) the bad. This might be an item, a tool, a promise, a scripture, a feeling, or a specific word.

9. What were the dangers of disobeying the Lord's command regarding the devoted things?

10. In addition to the total destruction of Jericho, Joshua cursed the city. What was the result of that curse? (See 1 Kings 16:34).

The Lord had given Jericho to the Israelites by a sovereign act of His power. This was His pledge that the conquest of the Promised Land was His battle, to be done His way. In return, He expected absolute obedience and loyalty. His battle, His rules.

The Israelites were required to *wait* to receive the spoils of battle. At long last they were in the Promised Land and had conquered a major city. Yet even now, they were commanded to remember the Lord's laws regarding the firstfruits. After 40 years of wandering, this must have been agonizing. It would be easy under these circumstances for impatience to reign.

MEMORY VERSE: *Deuteronomy 7:9*
Therefore know that the LORD your God, He is God, the faithful God who keeps covenant and mercy for a thousand generations with those who love Him and keep His commandments.

Keys To Conquering My Giant From This Lesson

Consider how you can apply what you've learned in Week 6 as you continue to conquer your giant.

ACTION ITEMS

A.

B.

C.

Notes & Prayer Requests

WEEK 7

FACING THE CONSEQUENCES

Consequences—the almost inescapable result of disobedience.[49] Sometimes, those consequences affect innocent people. Sometimes, they shake or even shatter our faith in God. Sometimes, they tempt us to take matters into our own hands.

Joshua and the entire community of Israelites suffered the consequences of one man's disobedience. The results were painful, even horrifying. But through the experience, the nation learned a greater reliance on their God.

---

[49] While there are generally consequences to our disobedience, there is also forgiveness and restoration in the LORD. (See 1 John 1:9). However, other humans may not be so ready to forgive and forget. And that might be one of the consequences of our disobedience.

Getting Started

1a. Describe a time in the past when your disobedience resulted in the punishment of or pain to another (innocent) person.

b. Why did you allow this to happen? How did you feel?

We shall seek the truth and will endure the consequences.[50]
~Charles Seymour

Background

The second fortress the Israelites took as they progressed towards the interior of the land was the city-state of Ai.[51] The country was divided into small territories, each under an independent chieftain or "king," who reigned in each fortified city and the district around it. Therefore, conquering the Promised Land would require a series of sieges rather than just one pitched battle.

Chapter 6 ends on a high point: "So the LORD was with Joshua, and his fame spread throughout the land" (Joshua 6:27). But the story immediately takes an unexpected and dreadful turn.

---

[50] Charles Seymour, an American historian and diplomat. This statement was made while he was president of Yale University (1937-1950).

[51] Ai (הָעַי, pronounced *hā'Ay*, means "the heap (of ruins)." ("Ai," Wikipedia accessed 2023_08_29, https://en.wikipedia.org/wiki/Ai_(Canaan).)

Read Joshua 7

"But the Israelites acted unfaithfully in regard to the devoted things …" (Joshua 7:1). Tragically, the disobedience of one man brought destruction on the whole nation.

> ### A BIT OF HISTORY
>
> Ai, situated on a conical hill about ten miles west of Jericho, was a much smaller city of only 12,000 inhabitants (see Joshua 8:25). Yet its position was exceedingly important. To the south, it opened the road to Jerusalem, only a few hours away. To the north, it commanded access to the heart of the country so that a victorious army could march unopposed into the fertile district of Samaria. Moreover, the fate of Ai also virtually decided that of nearby Bethel.
>
> The latter city, ruled by a different independent "king," lay to the west of Ai, separated from it by a high intervening hill. This hill, about midway between Bethel and Ai, was the site of Abram's altar when he first entered the land (see Genesis 12:8). Here also the patriarch had stood with Lot overlooking the rich Jordan valley when Lot made his choice of residence (see Genesis 13:3-11).

Sin cannot escape God's watchful eye, and it never affects only the sinner. This principle is woven throughout Scripture, beginning with Genesis and ending with Revelation. God's people are a covenant community, and what affects one affects all.

2a. Where else do you see this same principle (see Romans 5:12-19)? What impact did the sin of one man have on humankind?

b. How was that sin eventually atoned for? What was required?

In the full scope of the treasures, what Achan took was minor. Who would miss one Babylonian robe, two hundred shekels of silver, and fifty shekels of gold?[52] But the LORD had required *all* of Jericho's treasure to be devoted, and this seemingly "minor" sin resulted in great consequences.

3a. How did Achan's sin resemble that of Eve (see Genesis 3:6 and Joshua 7:21)?

> *I saw it.*
> *I wanted it.*
> *I took it.*

b. Do you think God really cared about the items Achan took? What was the real issue?

Elsewhere in the Old Testament, the word translated disgraceful (*nevalah*) is used almost exclusively for sexual sin. Achan had prostituted himself to the gods of Canaan and therefore had committed adultery in relationship to the LORD. God considered this violation of the covenant as a breaking of marriage vows, a critical sin the Israelites would continue to commit. But it wasn't his sin alone. The idea of covenant assumes "collective accountability." Achan's sin violated the covenant relationship God had with Israel, which was both corporate and individual. The

---

[52] That is, about 100 ounces of silver, 25 ounces of gold, and an ornate robe that a royal or high-ranking official might wear on a formal occasion. (Church, 221.). Keller puts the value of his spoil at about $25,000 in today's value. (Keller, 103.).

relationship with the whole was broken until the violation was atoned for by the individual responsible.[53]

4a. What were the consequences of this sin for Achan and his family?

b. What were the consequences of Achan's sin for Israel?

c. Do you think the same principle might apply to the Body of Christ today? What might be the consequences?

5a. Do you ever give in to the temptation to compromise with God? To cut corners or only to partially obey?

b. How might this pattern be strengthening your giant?

---

[53] NavPress (Firm), *A Life-Changing Encounter with God's Word from the Book of Joshua* (Colorado Springs: NavPress, 1988), 84.

The greater victory, the greater the temptation. Be careful when life is going well. It's easy to take God for granted, to rationalize our behavior, and soon fall into sin.

When the people learned of the presence of sin in the camp, Achan could have come forward and repented immediately. But even as the lots were being drawn and the circle narrowed around him, he chose to continue in his lie. His refusal to repent suggests he underestimated God's holiness and the severity of his sin. Or perhaps he was just confident he wouldn't be caught.

6a. Is it possible you have a secret sin, hidden from your friends and even your family, that is hindering your progress in conquering your giant(s)? If so, what is it, and how should you respond? Be honest. Now is the time to trust your group and allow them to help you.

b. Read 2 Samuel 11:1-12:15. What did David do to try to hide his sin? What was the consequence? Who was harmed in the process?

c. Meditate on Psalm 51 this week. David wrote this Psalm because of the incident with Bathsheba and all that followed. What new meaning do you see in it?

GIANT KILLING STRATEGY
CONFESSION AND REPENTANCE

It's human nature to cover up a sin. Children seem to learn this behavior by the time they can talk. In fact, sometimes it's amusing to watch them wiggle in an untruth. But as adults, we need to learn the skills of confession and repentance, both with one another and with the Lord.

God has given each of us a conscience. Unless we have dulled it by repeated disobedience, we know when we have sinned. And like Adam and Eve, we immediately resort to hiding. Lying. Blaming. Trying to cover up the sin. It won't work. At least, not for long and not if we want to be in relationship with God. But these behaviors are often anchors that keep a giant empowered.

If you want to conquer your giant, be swift to confess to God and others affected. Be willing to admit when you're wrong. Speak it out loud, in person if possible. Then repent. Apologize and ask for forgiveness.

The Hebrew word for repent is shuv. It means to make a U-turn. To stop doing what you were doing, to turn around and to go in the opposite direction. It does no one any good to say, "Sorry" and then keep on sinning. If we are truly sorry, it requires a change of behavior and mindset.

7a. Despite his personal and professional feelings, how did Joshua accuse Achan? What does this suggest about Joshua as a person and as a leader?

b. When you discover a friend, family member, or colleague in a sin, how should you respond? (See Galatians 6:1). What actions might this involve? Are you willing to be a Nathan to a friend, or perhaps to someone in your group? (See 2 Samuel 12:1-7).

Seventeenth-century clergyman John Donne wrote, "No man is an island entire of itself." His point was that we are all part of one another. We do not sin in isolation. What one person does touches the lives of others, either for good or evil. When one person sins, we are all diminished. The Israelite community learned that all too well.

It appears that Joshua sent the spies to Ai without inquiring of the LORD. Had he become presumptuous or overconfident after the great success at Jericho? Had the spies also become overconfident? Perhaps they felt that this was to be a minor skirmish—nothing significant enough to bother the LORD.

8a. How often do you try to do things on your own strength, especially if it's something you're good at or trained for or something that seems insignificant? What areas do you recognize are particularly vulnerable to this oversight?

b. Why is it wrong to consider any battle or decision insignificant? With whom is our battle (see Ephesians 6:12)?

c. How does God recommend that we prepare for warfare (see Ephesians 6:13-18, 2 Corinthians 10:4-5)?

The defeat at Ai was relatively minor—only 36 of 3,000 men were killed. But before he even knew what the problem was and before inquiring of the Lord, Joshua jumped to invalid conclusions and sounded remarkably like the fickle prior generation that Moses had led.

We tread on dangerous turf when we decide an action is too insignificant to bother the Lord or that we can handle this one on our own.

9a. How did Joshua respond to the defeat at Ai? For what was he willing to settle?

b. How does he assume this one defeat will affect the conquest? What else is he concerned about?

c. When you face defeat, are you concerned about God's reputation—or only your own?

10a. Is Joshua's response a common reaction in the face of strong opposition, fear, or defeat? Consider Elijah's response in I Kings 19:1-10. How does God respond in each case?

b. As you have faced your giant(s) in the past few weeks, has a small defeat caused you to have a "pity party" or to allow despair or discouragement to creep in? If so, what was the occasion and the cause?

> *Even in a minor defeat, it's easy to allow fear to overcome reason and despair to overcome faith.*

c. Did you seek the LORD immediately prior to the defeat? In retrospect, did you draw invalid conclusions? What voices were you listening to?

d. What might be the benefit of the despair and pain we feel when we face defeat?

Even good men, when things go against them a little, are too apt to fear the worst. [54]

~Matthew Henry

---

[54] Church, 220.

Compromise and presumption are two sins with serious consequences, including but not limited to defeat and discouragement. Joshua and the Israelites experienced both. Yet the LORD did not leave them or forsake them. When they repented, He restored them. We, too, must be willing to repent quickly of our sin and move on in the conquest of our giants.

MEMORY VERSE: *Psalm 51:10-12*
Create in me a clean heart, O God,
And renew a steadfast spirit within me.
Do not cast me away from Your presence,
And do not take Your Holy Spirit from me.
Restore to me the joy of Your salvation,
And uphold me by Your generous Spirit.

Keys To Conquering My Giant From This Lesson

Consider how you can apply what you've learned in Week 7 as you continue to conquer your giant.

ACTION ITEMS

A.

B.

C.

Notes & Prayer Requests

WEEK 8
WINNING GOD'S WAY

Obedience takes time. And commitment. And humility. Especially when we've just disobeyed and then must face the human objects of that disobedience again. That's what Joshua had to do in facing the city of Ai for the second time after dealing with Achan's sin. He couldn't afford to move ahead of God again.

Obedience also results in victory. Following God's strategy can be exciting if we're willing to set aside our own plans and agenda. In obeying God's strategy for Ai, Joshua not only won another victory but also regained the confidence of the Israelites.

And true obedience should culminate in only one thing—true worship. For when we obey, we see God as He is. And when we see God as He is, our natural response is to worship Him.

Getting Started

1. Describe a time in your past when you were defeated or embarrassed, and then had to return to that same setting again within hours or days. How did you feel? What happened?

Doing the will of God leaves me no time for disputing about His plans.

~George McDonald (1824-1905)

Background

Once they had discovered the cause of the initial defeat at Ai, Israel's prompt action was a form of corporate repentance. They acted quickly to obey God's requirements, even though that action was painful for many. With the sin of Israel removed, the covenant was restored. God once again assured Joshua of His presence and gave him the exact battle plan. Even though Joshua and Israel had sinned and experienced the tragic consequences of that sin, God did not forsake them.

Read Joshua 8:1-29

The strategy God ordered was unusual from three perspectives. First, Joshua was told to take his entire army—about 600,000[55] men to defeat 12,000. Second, it

---

[55] Based on the census of fighting men taken by Moses (Numbers 26).

was not to be a frontal attack of power, but rather a secretive ambush—a strategy usually reserved for the underdog. Joshua, freshly repentant, did not argue with these humiliations. And third, the Lord told Joshua to stretch out his spear toward Ai (see Joshua 8:18), just as Moses had stretched out his spear toward the formidable Red Sea. Joshua kept the spear stretched out until the army had utterly destroyed Ai, just like Moses (see Joshua 8:26).

2a. What reminder did God once again give Joshua?

b. What was God's timeframe for giving them victory this time? (See v. 1). What does this mean? How might this encourage Joshua and the army?

c. As you have faced your giant(s) and perhaps experienced a defeat during the past few weeks, perhaps you also need this word of encouragement. Rewrite these encouraging words, addressing them to yourself and your giant.

d. Having received the firstfruits, what did God now allow the Israelites to keep? What might that communicate to the nation?

God told Joshua His strategy for this battle and, in doing so, once again demonstrated His creativity. Each city, each battle, was to be different. And yet, God still wanted to be in control, even of the details.

> *When we honor God with the firstfruits, He is quick to be generous to us with His gifts.*

3a. As you face your giant(s), are you willing to seek God's strategy for each step in defeating them? Or, knowing the ultimate goal, do you tend to take the method into your own hands?

b. If you, like most of us, are prone to rushing ahead and presuming we know the plan, what will it take for you to change that habit? You will most likely need the help of your group for this one. And they'll need your help. Make a specific plan for learning to listen and wait on God's plans.

c. Where are you most vulnerable to rushing ahead or concocting your own strategy? For example, is it when you're doing something you know or are trained for? Is it when you know you have the spiritual gifting to do the task? Is it when you want to impress others or are afraid of their judgment? How can you apply this knowledge to conquering your giant?

Joshua had now gained confidence as a leader (v. 8) and the warriors had complete confidence in him. He had earned their respect by his faith in and obedience to God.

4a. Are you willing to pay your dues in the skirmishes of life to gain credibility in your circle of influence? Describe how you are doing or have done this.

b. Do people follow you because of your popularity, your competence, or because they recognize an obedient servant of the LORD? (You don't have to lead a congregation to be a leader. We are all leaders or influencers in some way.)

Read Joshua 8:30-35 and Deuteronomy 11:29-31

Obedience to the command of worship took both time and effort. Rather than moving forward to the next conquest as they surely were ready to do, they went back toward Gilgal (see map) to the designated mountains to offer sacrifices and to again read the law—the blessings and the curses, as Moses had commanded in Deuteronomy 27. These were the same sacrifices offered at Mt. Sinai when Moses received the covenant (see Exodus 20:24). This represented another renewal of the covenant.

> *To overcome, we must trust and obey. There is no other way.*

Six tribes stood on Mt. Ebal, and six stood on Mt. Gerizim, with the priests and the ark in the valley between them. When the priests read the blessings promised for keeping the covenant, the tribes on Mt. Gerizim assented with a loud "Amen!" When the priests read the curses promised for breaking the covenant, the tribes on Mt. Ebal echoed with "Amen!" The conical shape of the area created superb acoustical conditions so that all the tribes could clearly hear all that was read. The location was also strategic. From the top of either mountain, they could see all the Promised Land. Being located dead center of Canaan, these mountains represented the whole of the land to the Hebrew mind.[56]

A BIT OF HISTORY

God required that altars to Him be built of uncut stones (see Exodus 20:25). Cutting with tools would defile the altar, perhaps because using cut stones was a Canaanite practice or perhaps because it symbolized human effort, neither of which God wanted on His altar. Cutting stones also came dangerously close to carving an idol or graven image. God wanted to supply the materials for his altars uncut, just as He had created them.

After the nation had completed their worship, they were to build altars of uncut stone and offer sacrifices to the LORD, just as their parents had done at Mt. Sinai. Following the sacrifice, Moses had commanded that they whitewash the altar and write the law on it (see Deuteronomy 27:4-8).

---

[56] Jensen, 76.

5a. Have you developed the habit of worshipping the LORD after a partial victory, or do you wait until the battle is complete? The Israelites were only at the beginning of what would be a very long conquest. Yet they stopped to remind themselves of the covenant and to worship the covenant maker. What changes do you need to make in your habits to remember to thank the LORD for partial victories?[57]

> **GIANT KILLING STRATEGIES**
> **PRAISE AND WORSHIP AS A WEAPON**
>
> Do you ever wish you could take the Presence of God into your battles, just as the Israelites did with the Ark of the Covenant? Do you ever wish the Lord would fight for you, just as He did for Joshua? Well, you can, and He does.
>
> We see numerous examples in Scripture where a battle was fought through praise and worship rather than warfare. A great example is 2 Chronicles 20 where King Jehoshaphat and the people worshipped, and the Lord fought the battle for them. Psalm 2:3 tells us that the Lord inhabits the praises of His people.
>
> Instead of pleading with God, try praising and worshipping. Satan hates it, and God loves it. You will come away strengthened and fortified for what lies ahead.

---

[57] For us, worship may or may not take the form of music. Worship means to ascribe to the Lord the glory of his name. Psalm 29:2 (ESV) says,
> Ascribe to the LORD the glory due his name;
> worship the LORD in the splendor of holiness.

Praise and worship don't need to be anything formal, but the Psalms are a good place to start. Perhaps you just write today's victories in a gratitude journal. Perhaps it's just whispering a quick thank you as you go through your day. The key is to begin to train yourself to remember the LORD in everything you do.

b. We no longer make altars for animal sacrifice to the LORD. What might be an altar you could erect for worship, and how might you make sure it doesn't represent your human striving or skill? (This may or may not be a physical altar. It may be a mindset where you sacrifice a habit or sin pattern.)

6a. After you have learned a lesson of obedience and experienced its fruits, how do you take time to renew and refresh your relationship with the LORD? Do you take time not only to say "Thanks" but also to *worship* Him? If not, why not?

b. What form does your worship take? What do you find most effective in drawing near to God? Share your preferences with your group and learn from theirs.

c. Take time this week to stop and worship God, even though your giant still looms in front of you. Recount your praise for what you have learned and for the victories you have experienced to date in conquering your giant(s).

Man's chief end is to glorify God, and to enjoy Him forever.[58]
~ Westminster Shorter Catechism

Once again, Joshua and the Israelites were poignantly reminded of Who was responsible for their victorious invasion of the Promised Land. Each step needed to be accomplished strictly according to God's plan, in perfect obedience to Him. Once they understood this, their response was not rebellion, but *worship*. As we continue the process of conquering our personal giants, such a response will not only please the LORD, but will also encourage us for the next step.

MEMORY VERSE: *Psalm 95:6 (KJV)*
Oh come, let us worship and bow down; Let us kneel before the LORD our Maker.

---

[58] Westminster Shorter Catechism.

Keys To Conquering My Giant From This Lesson

Consider how you can apply what you've learned in Week 8 as you continue to conquer your giant.

ACTION ITEMS

A.

B.

C.

Notes & Prayer Requests

WEEK 9

DUPED BY DECEPTION

Deception. It's a ploy almost as old as mankind. Since the garden drama between Eve and the serpent, we have been vulnerable to deceit—and have ourselves been guilty of deceiving others. Men and women play games in relationships. Corporate officials deceive employees and stockholders. Politicians create facades to gain voters.

Why does deception continue to thrive? Have we learned nothing in the centuries since the garden? And more importantly, why do we continue to fall for it? Perhaps, like the Israelites, we consider most matters too insignificant to bother God with. Perhaps, like the Israelites, we think we are wise enough to handle everyday events on our own.

Deception often plays a role in breaking an agreement as well. Sometimes we just flat-out ignore a promise, especially an informal one with family or friends. But if the agreement is a formal contract, we may need to resort to a ruse to try to escape it. In any case, it's tempting to act less than honestly.

Getting Started

1. Consider a time in your past when you used deception to get what you wanted. What happened? What lesson did you learn (good or bad)?

Appearances are often deceiving.[59]
~Aesop

Background

With two major victories behind them, sin cleansed from the camp, and the covenant renewed, the Israelites prepared to continue their conquest of the land. Meanwhile, five neighboring kings, having first heard of and now *seen* of the power of the LORD, were quaking in fear. Knowing that divided they had no hope, these kings formed an alliance, hoping to rout Joshua's army.

However, the inhabitants of Gibeon[60] had a different and perhaps more prudent plan (see Joshua 9).

The Israelites were particularly vulnerable at this time. They had just returned from a successful do-over and a powerful time of worship, as they were reminded of the

---

[59] Aesop from *"The Wolf in Sheep's Clothing."*
[60] Gibeon was a Hivite royal city somewhat larger than Ai and about twenty miles from the Israelite camp at Gilgal. The Hivites are listed in Deuteronomy 20:17 as one of the nations God told the Israelites to totally destroy because of their pagan practices.

consequences of obedience and disobedience. Because it was a time of triumph, it was also a time of spiritual vulnerability.

Read Joshua 9

2a. What was the ruse to which the Gibeonites resorted?

b. Why do you think they chose this rather than joining the alliance of kings? What might they have learned as the priests read all the words of the law on Mts. Ebal and Gerizim (see Joshua 8:34, Deuteronomy 7:1-5)?

c. Why do you think they resorted to deception rather than being honest with the Israelites?

d. Is it possible that your giant is entrenched because of a deceptive practice? For example, are you deceiving yourself by lying or making excuses regarding why you're still dealing with this issue? Do you ever try to make yourself look better (more successful, more accomplished, more under control) than you are?

e. What do you think would happen if you just came clean with yourself and others, and admitted the truth about your giant? How would you feel? How do you think others would react? Is that true?

f. Have you been deceived by others or by Satan into making an ungodly alliance? How might that be affecting the conquering of your giant?

The Gibeonites sought to make a covenant with the Israelites. In this case, the Gibeonites were acting pre-emptively, hoping to cut their losses. Hoping to live.

> *If we follow the LORD into the battles He has chosen for us, it should create a fear of the LORD in others.*

The Hebrew word for covenant in verse 6 is the same word used for the Israelites' covenant with the LORD. In verse 15, it says they *"cut a covenant"* with the Gibeonites—exactly the same process as Abraham did with the LORD in Genesis 15:18.

The Gibeonites were not interested in serving the Hebrew God or living by His precepts. They were simply interested in saving their own skins, and it appears they succeeded. Joshua and his leaders made a "treaty of *shalom* (peace)" with the Gibeonites. A treaty to let them live. And as we will see in the next chapter, much more. The text specifically says, "but they did not ask counsel of the LORD" (Joshua 9:14).

A BIT OF HISTORY

In the Ancient Near East (ANE), it was common for one nation to become the vassal or servant of another, either voluntarily or as a consequence of war. Such agreements were called suzerain vassal covenants in acknowledgment of the superior position of one party and the inferior position of the other. The terms of the covenant were set by the sovereign and could be generous or repressive.

Every covenant contained at least three elements: 1) an affirmation or a promise, 2) a description of the responsibilities of each party, and 3) an appeal to their god as all-powerful, all-knowing, and the punisher of falsehoods. Once the terms were agreed upon (or imposed), the parties would generally share a meal and then cut one or more animals in half lengthwise. Each party would walk between the pieces and declare that this would be his fate if he violated the covenant. This was called "cutting covenant" (kārat berît).

Oaths in the ANE always appealed to the highest authority or god of the human makers of the oath. This put the reputation of the god at risk if either party violated the agreement. (This is why Hebrews 6:13 says, "For when God made a promise to Abraham because He could swear by no one greater, He swore by Himself…").

Covenants or oaths of the type the Israelites swore with the Gibeonites were regarded as bonds of international security, and their infraction was not only grounds of international complaint but also an offense against divine justice. Oaths to either Jehovah or to heathen deities were treated as tests of allegiance to that deity (see Exodus 23:13, Deuteronomy 29:12). The sanctity of both covenants and by extension, oaths, was carefully outlined in the Law. Breaking either was strongly condemned (see Exodus 20:7, Leviticus 19:12). Therefore, once the Israelites had sworn an agreement with the Gibeonites, they were required to honor it. No do-overs.

3a. Why had the Lord forbidden the Israelites to make a treaty with the inhabitants of the land? (See Exodus 23:32-33, 34:12-17, Numbers 33:55-56, Deuteronomy 7:2-6).

b. Do similar prohibitions apply to Christians today? (See 2 Corinthians 6:14 - 7:1, James 4:4).

c. Are we really called to be different or unique in today's world? For what purpose? (See Matthew 5:13-16). How seriously do most Christians honor oaths and covenants today?

d. Besides marriage, to what other relationships, legal contracts, or informal agreements might this apply? Are you involved in such a relationship, contract, or agreement?

e. Why would God be concerned about our involvement in improper contemporary relationships?

f. Is it possible your giant is linked directly or indirectly to an improper alliance with unbelievers? (Think carefully—the influence of some alliances is very subtle.) Describe that alliance and how it is or could be a snare to you. (Think about your personal, business, church, and civic involvements.)

4a. What error did the men of Israel make? Had they made this error before? If so, when?

As aliens and strangers in this world, to consider any action or decision too insignificant to inquire of the Lord may open us to unpleasant consequences.

b. After all they had been through, how might this have happened? Do you see a similar tendency in yourself? Under what conditions?

c. In the face of the great conquests awaiting them, do you think they considered a treaty with a faraway nation very significant? Why or why not? (Consider your response in Lesson 6, #5a). Do you see a similar tendency in yourself?

d. Given the Lord's commands regarding making covenants with any Canaanite nation, how should Joshua and his leaders have responded to the Gibeonites' request?

> *The humiliating defeat at Ai should have taught Joshua and the leaders to take time to pray and seek the mind of the Lord. After all, the Lord was the commander of the army. But they walked by sight and not by faith, and unbelief has a hard time waiting.*[61]
> ~ *Warren W. Wiersbe*

e. Are there issues regarding your giant where you should respond in the same way? How do you know this?

5a. It is also possible that the Israelites were simply politely accommodating their guests in true Eastern hospitality,[62] little realizing or considering the consequences. Have you ever been trapped like this? Give an example.

---

[61] Warren W. Wiersbe, and Thomas Nelson Publishers., *The Essential Everyday Bible Commentary: With the Complete Text of the New King James Version* (Nashville: T. Nelson, 1993).
[62] Hospitality was built into Ancient Near Eastern (ANE) culture in a way we barely understand. It was a matter of great shame not to show hospitality to strangers.

> ## GIANT KILLING STRATEGY
> ## WALK IN TRUTH
>
> In Western 21st century culture, we've lost the importance of truth and honesty. Prior to the 1960s, it was common to hear, "A man's word is his bond." A handshake was as good as a contract.
>
> Sadly, we've sacrificed that ethos on the altar of expediency. We cut corners, cross our fingers, and consider our word a mere suggestion to be honored when convenient. Deception is considered good business.
>
> It must not be so among the people of God. If we hope to conquer our giants, we must become people of truth, justice, and integrity. We must discipline ourselves in honoring our commitments, even if it hurts. Consider if there are places where you have cut corners or been outright deceptive. If so, make restoration where you can. Ask forgiveness where you can. Repent. Make a U-turn. And then determine to walk in Truth, no matter what.

b. In our case, *we* are the aliens in this world (I Peter 2:11). We must not be sidetracked from our mission. How are we called to respond when dealing with unbelievers? (See Matthew 10:16).

So Israel, once a nation of slaves, now became slave masters. It had never been God's will for them to make slaves of any inhabitants of the Promised Land, but Joshua and his captains had failed both to remember their original mission and to seek the Lord's will in this matter. Furthermore, in direct disobedience, they made a treaty with a Canaanite nation.

> *Although God is eager to forgive an error in judgment or even a deliberate sin, you may still suffer the consequences. And it may likewise affect future generations.*

History would later show how very unwise this move had been. It carried generational consequences. Four hundred years later, Israel's first king, Saul, rashly decided to destroy some of the troublesome Gibeonites. The fateful consequence of this action was a three-year famine decades later during David's reign. When the LORD finally revealed the cause, David attempted to restore the covenant. The price of reconciliation was the murder of seven of Saul's male descendants (see 2 Samuel 21:1-9).

6a. When the Israelites discovered the truth about the Gibeonites, how did they respond?

b. What does this indicate about the seriousness with which they viewed their agreement?

c. How are Christians to view oaths or covenants? (See James 5:12, Matthew 5:33-37).

Because God considers vows so seriously, it is possible, even probable, that the impact of an oath made in a previous generation is still impacting you and may be empowering your giant. These might include:

- Deliberate oaths, as are often made in the occult. These include "deals with the devil" or promises to leverage a future generation for immediate gain. If you or your family were involved with Freemasonry or even college or other fraternal organizations, you might be at risk.
- Oaths of convenience, like the one the Israelites made. This might include business contracts, marriages, or trades.
- Accidental oaths made in the heat of a moment. These might include agreements made while intoxicated or in anger or fear.

God considers each equally valid. If an oath from a previous generation is afflicting you or your family unjustly, the good news is that Jesus Christ has already paid the price for the violation. It is up to us to appropriate that prepayment. Take some time alone or with a spiritual advisor and ask God if there are any oaths or covenants in your bloodline that have been violated or not fulfilled and that are impacting your ability to conquer your giant. If He reveals anything, you can

- forgive the person whose oath is impacting you,
- repent on behalf of the previous generation,
- come out of agreement with the oath by renouncing it,
- nail the oath to the cross, allowing Jesus to fulfill it.

You can then plead your case to God as the righteous judge and implore Him to rescind the oath and negate its consequences since it is affecting you unjustly.[63] If you have personally made such an oath, you may be able to repent, or you may need to fulfill it. This will be a serious conversation between you and God and probably a spiritual advisor.

7a. Is there an oath or vow you made in your past against which you are chafing? It is possible that oath or vow is related to giants yet unconquered. What is it? What does God say about it?

b. Knowing how seriously God considers oaths, how will you act to honor that promise this week?

c. Is it possible there is an oath made by someone in a previous (or current) generation that is holding your giant in place? You might need to do some investigating, or you might simply ask God what it is. You could be surprised by what you learn.

---

[63] For more on this concept, see *Accessing the Courts of Heaven: Positioning Yourself for Breakthrough and Answered Prayers,* Robert Henderson, Destiny Image Publishers, 2017.

It's easy to be seduced by the deception of the world. Because Joshua and the Israelites did not carefully consider the implications of their actions, both they and their future generations paid heavily for their carelessness.

MEMORY VERSE: *James 5:12*

But above all, my brethren, do not swear, either by heaven or by earth or with any other oath. But let your "Yes" be "Yes," and your "No," "No," lest you fall into judgment.

Keys To Conquering My Giant From This Lesson

Consider how you can apply what you've learned in Week 9 as you head into the home stretch to conquer your giant.

ACTION ITEMS

A.

B.

C.

Notes & Prayer Requests

CONFRONTING A GANG OF GIANTS

Faithfulness.

A quality we desire, admire, covet, seek—in God and in our friends. A quality we strive to build in ourselves—in relation to God and to our associates.

One of the great joys of life is knowing, beyond a shadow of a doubt, that we have someone we can count on, night or day, through thick and thin. One of the great tragedies of life is feeling we are all alone and have no one to turn to.

Nothing brings these truths more alive than an urgent need. A need that I know I can't handle alone. That's when the mettle of a friendship or covenant is tested. That's when our character is tested. And that's when our faith in God is tested.

Getting Started

1. Do you have a friend you can call at any time of the day or night and know for sure that he or she will respond? Who is it? What has forged this level of commitment?

A friend in need is a friend indeed.[64]
~Richard Graves

Background

As always seems to happen, when God's person is experiencing victory, the challenges increase. The action of the Gibeonites and the demonstrated faithfulness of God to His people caused the kings of southern Canaan, led by the king of Jerusalem[65], to join forces. Perhaps in assessing the situation, they decided that if a city as strong and well-fortified as Gibeon would seek the safety of a peace treaty, the smaller towns had no chance, for Gibeon was a powerful and significant royal city. Her surrender left a dangerous gap in the defense of the South, giving Israel a strong position in the heart of the country within easy reach of Jerusalem. But rather than attacking the Israelites, the coalition attacked Gibeon!

---

[64] *Richard Graves (1715 - 1804)*
[65] His name was *'adonai 'tzedeq* which means Lord of Righteousness.

There are at least three reasons this made sense:

- First, it was an act of revenge for Gibeon's betrayal of the Canaanite coalition by providing a base for the Israelites within their own area.[66]
- Second, it would test the quality of the Israelites' treaty with Gibeon and either draw them into the conflict so the alliance could kill both birds with one stone or it would demonstrate that the Israelites' promises were worthless.[67]
- Third, Israelite possession of the passes leading from Gibeon would throw the whole south of Canaan open to their intrusion.

Under the circumstances, it was natural that the chieftains of the South would combine to retake Gibeon. The march of the combined kings was evidently rapid and seemed to have found the Gibeonites unprepared. Their appeal for immediate assistance was urgent.

Read Joshua 10:1-16

Matthew Henry suggests that some of the warriors of Israel might have considered Joshua's slowness and prudence as cowardice. After all, so far, they had conquered Jericho by a miracle, Ai by strategy, and Gibeon by surrender. That was all. But Canaan was not to be conquered in a day. The plan for the progressive conquest of Canaan had been divinely determined for Israel before she ever arrived in the land.[68] Even before the 40 years in the wilderness, the LORD, knowing the number of Israelites would be small, had designed a plan to protect the land from desolation

---

[66] ———, *Preaching the Word Commentary*, Accordance edition hypertexted and formatted by OakTree Software, Inc., Version 1.5 ed. (Wheaton, Illinois: Crossway Books).

[67] ———, *Preaching the Word Commentary*.

[68] Church, 225.

by nature. He had said, "little by little" (see Exodus 23:30, Deuteronomy 7:22),[69] so Joshua waited for the Canaanites to become the aggressors.

His opportunity came when the five kings joined forces against the Gibeonites. But this opportunity also offered a challenge. The two previous battles had been against single cities. Could the Israelites stand against such a strong coalition?

2a. Why do you think the five kings felt they needed to join forces? Was this a valid consideration?

b. Do you ever feel as if you are being attacked by a coalition of evil? Give an example from your experience where the enemy attacked your weakness instead of your strength.

3a. How did the Gibeonites deal with this threat? Why did they feel this freedom?

b. When one giant or a coalition threatens you, what is your typical response? Why?

---

[69] We will discuss this concept more in the next lesson.

4a. Verse 8 suggests that Joshua might have been afraid of what lay ahead. Why might he still be experiencing fear? Do you find it surprising that a person with so much trust in God would still be fearful?

> *When our spiritual enemies set themselves in array against us and threaten to swallow us up, let us, by faith and prayer, apply to Christ, our Joshua, for strength and succor...* [70]
> ~Matthew Henry

b. In what areas do you still experience fear, discouragement, or despair as you face your giant(s)? What does the Lord say to you? Rewrite verse 8 to apply it to your situation.

Joshua may also have felt frustrated that this battle was being forced on him because of his foolish mistake. But here we again see the Lord's graciousness as He turned Joshua's error into an opportunity to conquer five enemy cities in one day.

5a. As you have faced your giant(s) these past several weeks, have you made a mistake you thought was irredeemable? What was it? How has God responded to you? If He hasn't already, is it possible God can use even this in your quest to conquer your giant(s)? (See Romans 8:28).

---

[70] Church, 225.

Joshua lost no time in responding to Gibeon's cry for help. He pushed his army to the max. The road from Gilgal to Gibeon was twenty-six miles with a rise of about 3,300 feet,[71], but his army covered that distance in one night, which is compared with the standard of three days most Eastern armies would take to cover the same distance.[72] The exhausted army immediately attacked, catching the opposition by surprise. And then, they had to keep on fighting for an extremely long day.

6a. Since God had promised victory, why did Joshua need to tire himself and his army by marching all night? Why not wait until morning after a good night's sleep?

b. Given Joshua's response, what might be *your* responsibility when you appeal to Christ for help? Are you willing to persevere until the task is accomplished?

c. You've been taking aim at your giant for a couple of months now. Have you grown weary on your mission? (See 2 Thessalonians 3:13). Is it possible that a lackadaisical attitude on your part is slowing the conquest of your giant? If you aren't sure, consider inviting others in your group to provide their observations.

---

[71] Kenneth and John R. Kohlenberger III (Consulting Editors) Baker, ed., *Expositor's Bible Commentary Abridged Edition-Two Volume Set (NIV Commentary)* (Grand Rapids, MI: Zondervan, 1994), 1, 6.

[72] Robert Jamison, Fausset, A.R., and David Brown, *Jamison Fausset and Brown's Commentary Critical and Explanatory on the Whole Bible* (Accordance Bible Software, Oaktree Software, Inc., 1871), 2.6.

d. Are you figuratively marching uphill all night to conquer your giant(s)? Or are you taking your time, enjoying the sights along the way? What is motivating that choice?

GIANT KILLING STRATEGY
EVERY 37 SECONDS

Slaying a giant is seldom a one-step process. It takes diligent focus and repetition. Conquering fear is only one step, but it's an important one.

One of my favorite strategies is "Every 37 Seconds." Why? Because that's about how often fear hits me in the gut when I'm fighting a giant. The minute I feel fear anywhere in my body or mind, I rehearse the Truth from Scripture. I may need to write out a few verses so I can speak them out loud, with gusto, the minute fear tries to attack.

I learned this as a young mom, having just closed my business to raise my son. Because of my background of growing up poor, I was convinced that if I stopped working, we would starve! Literally! I had images of Hagar watching her son die in the desert. This fear came out as a wail and scared even me. But I knew my God and His promises, so I talked back. Every 37 seconds, or whenever the fear hit.

I would say, out loud and with gusto, "That's a lie! My God won't allow us to starve. He's Jehovah Jira, our provider, and He will provide for us!" Then I'd go about my business—for about 37 seconds until that spirit of fear would attack again. I'd speak God's Truth from the Word out loud, again and again and again. But in about a month, that spirit of fear left, and I never again feared poverty.

Verses 11-14 describe two great and unusual natural events. First, the LORD confounded the enemy with hailstones so large they could kill a man. Then, at Joshua's request, "the sun stood still" until the battle could be won. There have been many attempts to explain this phenomenon, but the point is that the LORD intervened miraculously.

> *An important fact that should not be overlooked is that the sun and moon were principal deities among the Canaanites. It may have seemed to the Canaanites that even their gods were compelled to obey when the leader of the Israelites prayed.*[73]
> ~Donald Campbell

6a. Describe a time when "the sun stood still" for you. Was this in relation to your giant or previously? If presently, how will this move you forward concerning your giant? If previously, how can that miracle inspire your faith for what is needed to conquer your giant?

b. Can we expect God to work miraculously in our battle to conquer our giants? (See Ephesians 3:20). Do you really believe this? Ask in expectant faith for a much-needed intervention in your struggle today.

---
[73] Campbell, 82.

A BIT OF HISTORY

It was a common ancient custom for the victorious kings to put their feet upon the necks of the conquered enemies. The purpose was to publicly humiliate their foes. The ancients considered the foot to be the lowest part of the body in status as well as physically. The head (and after it, the neck) was the most honorable, exalted part of the body. So, this gesture implied that the enemy's most honorable parts were lower than the victor's least ones. It was also a type of Jesus' position in relation to his enemies. (See Psalm 110:1, 1 Corinthians 15:24-28, Ephesians 1:19-23).[74]

Read Joshua 10:16-27

Joshua's army captured, humiliated, and eventually put to death the five kings, the ringleaders of the rebellion. This was a major victory for Joshua and the Israelites in their conquest of the land of the giants.

7a. What was done to the five kings?

b. How did Joshua encourage his leaders as they faced the kings?

---

[74] ———, *A Navpress Bible Study on the Book of Joshua* (Colorado Springs, CO: NavPress, 1988), 110.

c. What was the purpose of publicly displaying the bodies of the kings?

d. Why was it equally important to take them down from the tree and cast them away?

A public display of a defeated giant can serve as an encouragement and faith builder, not only to ourselves but also to others. But, after an appropriate season, it is equally important to put the defeated giant to rest and move on to the next battle.

e. How have you given public display or testimony regarding the giants you have defeated during this study? How have you been willing to encourage others with your victories?

f. Are you still resting on those victories while the Lord has urged you to move on to the next one? If so, what needs to be done?

Read Joshua 10:29-43

Having conquered the leaders of the southern coalition, Joshua then proceeded to conquer each of their cities and others along the way. He destroyed the cities and everything in them, just as the LORD had commanded. The Lord was with him and gave him victory in every place he set his foot.

8. Sometimes, one victory leads to a cascade, almost as if that one obstacle had been holding everything else back. Have you experienced that yet in dealing with your giant? If so, describe what happened. If not, stay alert. It's likely to happen.

As he prepared to forge into the Promised Land, the Gibeonites tested Joshua's faithfulness, and he tested the LORD's faithfulness. Both passed the test. As we forge toward conquering our giants and our larger goal of being conformed to the image of Jesus Christ, we can also expect to find the LORD utterly faithful. The question is, will He find us faithful?

MEMORY VERSE: *Ephesians 3:20-21*
Now to Him who is able to do exceedingly abundantly above all that we ask or think, according to the power that works in us, to Him be glory in the church by Christ Jesus to all generations, forever and ever. Amen.

Keys To Conquering My Giant From This Lesson

Consider how you can apply what you've learned in Week 10 as you press into the home stretch to conquer your giant.

ACTION ITEMS:

A.

B.

C.

Notes & Prayer Requests

WEEK 11

TAKING THE OFFENSIVE

"Problems? We eat 'em for breakfast!" Don't you wish life were so simple? In this age of instant gratification, we somehow expect our problems to be solved instantly. In fact, we're amazed when, after a few days or weeks or even months or years, certain problems continue to haunt us. What went wrong?

Probably nothing.

As Joshua discovered, conquering giants takes a while! And conquering giants is often filled with surprises. Even today, most giants are not conquered just as we expect them to be. They grow, shrink, change character, and generally bewilder us. Yet we somehow assume that God, like a magic genie, will simply erase the problem and eradicate the giant from the face of the earth. He may indeed do that, but such easy solutions are the exception rather than the rule. More frequently, God wants to change *us* rather than the giant. After all, one of His primary purposes is to conform *us* to the image of Jesus Christ, not just to vanquish another giant!

Getting Started

1. Recall a problem at home or work that looked simple until you started working on it but then seemed to swell like overactive bread dough.

The difficult we do immediately.
The impossible takes a little longer.[75]
~U.S. Army

Read Joshua 10:28-43

The death of the five Southern kings was only the beginning of a campaign that may have lasted for weeks or even months. It appears that the successors of these five kings later shared their fate.[76] The kings and armies of the cities had been overcome. Now there remained the actual conquest of the cities themselves in a geographically sensible progression.

The city of Makkedah was not part of the original coalition but simply had the ill fate of harboring the coalition kings. It was a minor enemy—one that perhaps could have survived a bit longer. But in aiding the five kings, it showed its potential against Israel. Joshua took the offensive and routed Makkedah on his way south.

---

[75] Slogan of the United States Army.
[76] Edersheim, 201.

2a. As you have been conquering your giant(s) during the past several weeks, have you discovered "contributing factors," that is, habits, decisions, attitudes, related areas of sin, or things from your past that aid or contribute to the entrenchment of those giants? What are they?

b. Ask your group for prayer and ask the LORD to help you overcome them. These insights may be a significant key to overcoming your giant(s).

As we begin to rout out the giants in our lives, the Lord will show us those peripheral areas of sin or bondage that also need to be dealt with.

3a. Identify Joshua's strategy on the map on page 17. What did he gain by attacking one city at a time?

b. How might this strategy apply to your giant(s)?

c. Although the original kings in the coalition were killed near Makkedah, successors were quickly appointed. Although not necessarily a spiritual principle, what parallel can you draw from this to your personal giants?

> *When the LORD identifies giants in our lives, and we give Him permission to work, He will continue the campaign to subdue them until they are defeated.*

d. Although the campaign continued for months or even years, verse 42 tells us, "All these kings and their lands Joshua conquered in *one* campaign, because the LORD, the God of Israel, fought for Israel." Describe the campaign you are now in and how the LORD your God is fighting for you. Name your giant(s) and describe the fate you are declaring for them.

Read Joshua 11

When Joshua returned to the camp at Gilgal, he was in control of the southern portion of the Promised Land. But he could not yet rest. The northern kings, hearing of Israel's victory in the South, also formed a coalition.

4a. What three frightening characteristics did this coalition boast?

   1.

   2.

   3.

b. As this even larger and more formidable giant loomed before them, how did the Lord encourage them?

 **A BIT OF HISTORY**

Horses and chariots were common in warfare in the Ancient Near East (ANE). Every Canaanite state had their chariots and charioteers to strike fear in their opponents.

Hamstringing horses was also common. It involved cutting their tendons above the hock (ankle) making it impossible for them to run. Although they were still able to be used as workhorses, they were no longer weapons.

In Deuteronomy 17:16, the Lord had commanded that when Israel got a king, he was not to accumulate horses. And later in Psalm 20:7, David reaffirmed:
>Some trust in chariots, and some in horses;
>But we will remember the name of the LORD our God.

This victory, like crossing the Jordan on dry land, was a repeat of the miracles experienced by the Exodus generation (see Exodus 14-15). The Lord was reminding them of His power and faithfulness to them.

c. Give two reasons why the LORD might order them to hamstring their horses and burn their chariots rather than appropriate them for battle.

1.

2.

d. What frightens you the most about your giant? How might you "hamstring" it or "burn" it to feel less threatened or overwhelmed?

e. What are the "horses and chariots" of your giant which, if they were available to you, you could easily begin to trust in?

Perhaps you have already conquered some giants during this study; perhaps you are still working on your first one. Either way, another giant, perhaps larger and more frightening than the first, probably lies ahead. This is not to discourage you but rather to help you realistically face the process of conquering the giants in your life. The good news is that the same God who went before Joshua is going before you!

5a. What might your newly formed "northern coalition" be?

b. Why do you feel you are being called to conquer this new or morphed giant? How do you feel about the prospect?

c. What do you know for sure about the battle and the outcome? (See Philippians 1:6).

GIANT KILLING STRATEGY
KILL THE "WHAT IFS"

In Lesson 1, we killed the "If Onlys"—the regrets that hold us hostage to the past. In this lesson, we'll attack the "What Ifs"—the fears that hold us hostage to the future. It's easy to get caught in the "what ifs" when facing the unknown. Imaginations soar as we consider every little thing that might hdix to harm or thwart us. The result is analysis paralysis. We're stopped cold in our tracks.

The remedy to the "what ifs" is just as easy as the "if onlys." Plan ahead. When fear besets you, look at the facts and figure out how you'll solve the problem, just in case it happens. Granted, most fears never materialize, but for the few that do, solve the problem in advance.

Decide, "If (problem happens…), I will (do this… to handle the problem) or (I will rest in the knowledge that God has this one handled beforehand)." Come up with your best ideas and decide in advance which you'll use. Rehearse it until you are confident, and let fear dissipate into thin air.

CONQUERING YOUR GIANTS

In verse 18, we learn that Joshua and his army resisted the temptation to settle down. They waged war against these kings for a long time. Most authorities agree that the time required to conquer the southern and northern kingdoms was between five and seven years. Some giants take a while to conquer. Some may not be totally conquered this side of eternity. So if you're still fighting, don't lose hope.

6a. Who is credited with the obstinacy of the northern tribes? Why?

b. What are some of God's major purposes in allowing His people to face hardship? (See Job 1:8-22, John 9:1-3).

c. Do you respond as Job did when you face setbacks? Are you glorifying God in your trials as well as your joys? If not, what changes do you need to make in your attitudes and behaviors?

These wars put Israel in possession of Canaan and broke the power of its inhabitants. But all the cities had not been taken, nor had all the inhabitants been exterminated. Practically speaking, that would not have been desirable. Moses had instructed them:

And the LORD your God will drive out those nations before you *little by little;* you will be unable to destroy them at once, lest the beasts of the field become too numerous for you. But the LORD your God will deliver them over to you and will inflict defeat upon them until they are destroyed (Deuteronomy 7:22-23, emphasis added).

7a. As you have been picking off your giant little by little, what have you encountered? Have you grown weary? Discouraged? Angry? Frustrated? Confess that to the LORD and receive fresh instructions, fresh determination, and a fresh infusion of hope.

b. What have been the benefits of conquering your giant(s) little by little?

> *To us also has our Joshua [Jesus] given entrance into Canaan, and victory over our enemies—the world, the flesh, and the devil. We have present possession of the land. But we do not yet hold all its cities, nor are our enemies exterminated. It needs on our part constant faith; there must be no compromise with the enemy, no tolerance of his spirit, no cession of our warfare. Only that which at first gave us the land can complete and consolidate our possession of it.[77]*
>
> ~Alfred Edersheim

---

[77] Edersheim, 202.

c. What are the risks of trying to conquer your giant(s) all at once? Have you experienced any of those?

Besides the practical, there was also a higher purpose to this plan of "little by little." It would teach the nation that a conquest, begun in the power of and dependence on the LORD, must be completed in the same spirit. Only then could Israel prosper as a nation. The LORD had given Canaan to Israel. But there was much left to be done, and that would require a continuation of a steady pace and the same level of faith.

The LORD had warned them. Any conformity to the nations around them, any tolerance of heathenism, or any dalliance with the pagan gods would result in the dilution of their purity and their eventual ruin. He said friendship or marriage with the Canaanites would become a snare to them (see Deuteronomy 7:16). The lesson of all this is obvious and critical. The Israelites would be required to repent of such behaviors many times during their history in the land.

Repenting is more than saying you're sorry. The Hebrew word for repent is *shuv*. It means to turn or return, or more literally, to make a U-turn. To turn around and go in the opposite direction. It's an action word and one of the most important words in the Hebrew language. It's used over 1,000 times in the Old Testament.

8a. As you have worked at conquering your giant(s) for these past months, where have you compromised or been tempted to compromise and befriend the enemy? Where have you been tempted to worship a god other than the LORD? (This might be a figurative befriending as you are lured into compromise or fantasy, habits or addictions. It might be a temptation to follow the ways of a "foreign god," AKA an idol.)[78]

b. What would it look like for you to repent? To make a U-Turn? Be specific. How would this move you forward in your quest to conquer your giant(s)? What will it take for you to make a U-turn and utterly change your behavior and attitude?

c. What do you need to do besides *shuv*? Is there an action you need to take with another person? Is there a habit you need to renounce and never engage in again? Is there restitution you need to make?

---

[78] "Foreign gods" don't necessarily need to carry foreign names. Some of our "foreign gods" are sex, money, power, pride, addictions, lust, envy…. The list fills the Bible.

When Joshua had taken the entire land, just as the LORD had directed Moses, he prepared to divide it among the tribes. Then the land had rest from war (see Joshua 11:23). How gracious is our LORD, who, after giving us victory, also gives us rest.

As Israel progressed into the Promised Land, Joshua found that each victory simply created new campaigns. Individual kings formed coalitions. His primitive army faced frightening weaponry. Yet as they were faithful to continue pressing on, God was faithful to give them the Promised Land, "little by little."

MEMORY VERSE: *Philippians 1:6*
Being confident of this, that he who began a good work in you will carry it on to completion until the day of Christ Jesus.

Keys To Conquering My Giant From This Lesson

Consider how you can apply what you've learned in Week 11 as you head into the home stretch to conquer your giant.

ACTION ITEMS:

A.

B.

C.

Notes & Prayer Requests

THE TWELVE TRIBES OF ISRAEL

WEEK 12
FACING CHANGE

Transition. Change. The very words upset our internal equilibrium. Change can be exciting or frightening, welcome or unwelcome, eagerly anticipated or reluctantly endured. The only thing we can be sure of is that things *will* change.

Joshua faced change. After half a lifetime of wandering in the desert and many years of leading fierce battles, he was now being called to a new way of life. Indeed, the very thing he had spent much of his life working for was about to come to pass.

How would this great leader face change? How would he handle the transition to life "behind the desk?" How would he accept those tasks that were yet unfinished and would now become the province of the younger men of the nation? How would he be able to let go of all he had overseen? The answers to these questions can offer some guidelines for each of us as we, too, face change.

Getting Started

1a. Recall a major change you faced in your childhood or early adulthood. What was it? Why was it important to you?

b. How did you handle it? What would you do differently if you could?

Changes [in life] are not only possible and predictable, but to deny them is to be an accomplice to one's own unnecessary vegetation.[79]

~Gail Sheehy

---

[79] Gail Sheehy, *Passages : Predictable Crises of Adult Life*, Ballantine Books Trade pbk. ed. (New York: Ballantine Books, 2006), 18.

Background

Approximately seven years had passed since Moses' death and the Israelites' entry into the Promised Land.[80] These had been years of testing, challenge, bloody battle, and repeatedly proving the Lord's faithfulness. As the land and the people rested from battle, Joshua chronicled their victories and faced new challenges.

Read Joshua 12-13[81]

Note that the first six verses of Chapter 12 chronicle in detail Moses's leadership in conquering the first giants. The following verses more briefly list the thirty-one kings defeated by Joshua and outline the territory taken. Even after all this time and after his own successes, Joshua neither forgets nor shortchanges Moses' memory.

Joshua was approximately 92 years old when the Lord gave him rest from battle. Caleb, the only other old man, was 85. The next oldest person could not have been over 65. Even as He gave them rest, the Lord reminded them of the lands yet untaken and promised to drive out some of the people Himself.

At long last, approximately 47 years after the exodus from Egypt, the tribes were to receive their inheritances. The tragedy is that Israel could have possessed her new homeland in just seven or eight years if she had responded in faith with Caleb and Joshua at Kadesh-Barnea. Instead, it took 47 years and the death of the unbelieving generation in the wilderness. What a price for unbelief!

---

[80] Caleb was 40 years old when he was sent as a spy into the Promised Land (see Joshua 14:7). The Israelites wandered in the wilderness for 38 years (see Footnote 14, Deuteronomy 2:14), which would have made him 78 when the conquest began. He was 85 when he demanded Joshua give him Hebron (see Joshua 14:10). Therefore, we can assume that the conquest of the South and the North took about seven years.

[81] In this and the subsequent chapters, don't get mired in the details. Look for the main points and interesting incidents. We are going to skim the rest of the book, not look at it in detail.

 **A BIT OF HISTORY**

Chapters 13-21 are written in the language of the formal land grant treaties of that day, where a king would distribute land to the loyal subjects who helped him conquer it. But unlike the Canaanite structure, where the king owned everything and the people only worked in the land as sharecroppers, the Israelite system gave ownership of a plot of land to each clan (a group of extended families) and to each family within the clan. Every 50 years, the land was redistributed within the clan according to the growth or shrinkage of families. It was illegal to sell land outside of the clan, and land could only be leased for up to 49 years. It had to be returned to the original owner in the year of Jubilee (see Leviticus 25:10, 14).

2. Make a list of the "kings" or giants you have defeated since becoming a Christian. In your list, give credit to others who have helped you in some significant way. Is there someone on that list who deserves special thanks? Why not call them or write a note this week?

> *All the land described by the LORD belonged by Divine gift to Israel. That it was still unoccupied by them, and that Joshua was now old, constituted the ground for the Divine command to make immediate distribution of the land among the tribes. It was as if, looking to His promise, God would have bidden Israel consider the whole land as theirs, and simply go forward, in faith of that promise and in obedience to His command.*[82]
> ~Alfred Edersheim

---
[82] Edersheim, 202.

3. What risk did the unconquered giants pose to the Israelites (see Numbers 33:55-56)? Apply this to your personal situation.

As Joshua faced this transition in his life, it is helpful to note several factors and apply them to our individual situations.

Joshua was perhaps not as healthy as Moses. Moses led his people in the wilderness until his death at age 120. He got no retirement, while God proposes at least a change of pace for Joshua (from military leader to administrator).

Since each person is unique, we must not compare ourselves with others. Rather we must accept the person God has created and called us to be.

4a. How did Joshua react to the LORD's suggestion of his age?

b. If you are over 50, are you willing to gracefully accept your aging process and accept those things you can no longer do? Are you willing to give up your exciting life as a warrior and gracefully step into a less demanding or different role? Or perhaps you are being called out of retirement and into active duty. What does transition mean to you at this point in your life?

> *Throughout our lives, as our heavenly Father sees our needs, our changing strengths and weaknesses, and our desires, He will lovingly call us from one way of life to another.*

God took notice of Joshua. He initiated the concern. Joshua continued "doing his job" until his loving Father, who gave him the battles, now gave him rest.

5a. Do you *really* believe that God takes notice of you and knows your needs even better than you do? (See Genesis 16:8-13, Matthew 6:32, Isaiah 65:24.) Do you *really* believe that He will not ask you to do more or fight more difficult battles than you can handle? Tell God how you feel about this.

b. Give an example of a time the LORD saw your need for a change of pace and gave it to you with no effort on your part. Did you consider this change something good or bad? When this change occurred, how did you react? Did you see it as from the hand of God?

Just as Joshua had led the nation in battle, he was now being asked to lead them in peace. The tribes had "matured" and were ready to be given their inheritances. They were ready to leave the security of the whole nomadic nation marching and living together.

6a. How might Joshua have felt as he was asked to divide the land and allow the tribes to go off and settle in their inheritances? (Remember that throughout the land there were cities and regions not yet conquered.)

Faith is like a muscle. It must be exercised to be fit. A life spent exercising faithful obedience gives God's person the maturity to choose to obey quickly, even when the command is not appealing.

b. How do you feel when you must relinquish someone or something you've nurtured to another? (This may be a child, a job, a disciple, a ministry, or anything else into which you have invested a great deal of love and concern.)

c. Could this have anything to do with your giant? Describe that connection.

Joshua needed to obey quickly. The LORD's sense of urgency did not allow time for "just one more battle."

A life of faithful obedience frees us from feeling driven to "do it all" or even "finish it all."

7a. Have you learned to obey quickly or are you still more likely to argue with the LORD about His commands and His timing?

b. Describe a time during this study when you clearly understood an urgent command from the LORD? How did you respond?

A mark of success is when you have worked yourself out of a job by helping others to become more mature.

Joshua had not finished conquering all the giants of the land. In fact, the LORD started the conversation by reminding Joshua, "You are old, advanced in years, and there remains very much land yet to be possessed" (Joshua 13:1-7). Then, He proceeded to list all the lands remaining to be taken.

8a. How do you reconcile this with Joshua 11:23?

b. How do you think Joshua felt as he realized how much remained undone?

c. Do you think the Lord was displeased as He listed the remaining lands? Why or why not? Were the lands unconquered because Joshua had failed or simply because the Lord had other plans?

d. Although Jesus had left many unhealed and multitudes unfed, what was He able to say as He hung on the cross? (see John 17 and 19:30).

e. You listed the giants in your life that remain to be conquered in Week 11. How do you feel about this unfinished business? How do your feelings about this affect your obedience? Do you need to confess or confront this?

f. Are you willing to leave the battle you are in when the Lord leads you to the next phase? What might this look like?

As the LORD listed the lands remaining, He also pointed out the dual responsibility of the Israelites and Himself.

9a. What did the LORD say He would do in verse 6b? What does this imply?

> *Sabbath shows us a God who knows when to stop. When to say "Enough."*[83]
>
> ~Marty Solomon

b. As you consider your giants yet unconquered, what is the LORD's responsibility? What is your responsibility? Are you willing to do your part to inherit your promised land (that is, to become conformed to the image of Jesus Christ)? Where do you need help or prayer?

c. Even as He expects us to diligently pursue the battles He sets before us, how has He prepared us? (See 2 Peter 1:3-11, Philippians 2:12).

---

[83] Marty Solomon, "Knowing When to Say 'Enough'," Season 1, Episode 2, in *BEMA Podcast*, https://www.bemadiscipleship.com/2.

This promise that He would drive them out from before the children of Israel plainly supposes it as the condition of the promise that the children of Israel must themselves attempt their extirpation, else they could not be said to be driven out before them; if afterwards Israel, through sloth or cowardice, sit still and let them alone, they must blame themselves and not God if they be not driven out. We must work out our salvation, and then God will work in us and work with us.[84]

~Matthew Henry

Background - Chapter 14

Joshua repeated the description of the lands given by Moses to the two-and-a-half tribes east of the Jordan. Before Joshua drew lots for the remaining tribes, Caleb requested his portion. Caleb, now 85, was still walking by faith and asked for a most difficult, heavily fortified, and largely unconquered land. He asked for the territory occupied by the very giants that, 47 years earlier,[85] had caused the other ten spies to quake in fear (Numbers 13). It was fitting that he be accorded this special honor.

Read Joshua 14

We haven't heard much about Caleb through the book of Joshua. It's as if he's been waiting behind the curtain or in the background for such a time as this. His name means "mad dog," which is a character trait important for both his past and his future.

---

[84] Church, 229.
[85] See Footnote 82.

10a. What did God say about Caleb in Numbers 14:24? What do you think this means?

b. What do we see in Caleb's character after all these years? What land did he request for his inheritance?

A life of faithful obedience in little things prepares the child of God to look beyond age or other human frailties and to continue to accept, even seek, greater challenges.

c. Do you have the faith to ask the LORD for the most difficult or challenging portion? What is that for you? Do you have any reason to believe you should have it?

In our lives, we will experience seasons of slavery to the world and its ways, times of wandering in the desert of our error, intervals of battles to conquer the giants, and interludes of rest in the land God has chosen for us to inherit. Through it all, our God is faithful!

d. What promise(s) are you standing on? What in your earlier life might have prepared you to be so bold?

e. Caleb, like Joshua and Moses, spent 38 years reaping the consequences of someone else's mistake. How would you respond in such a situation? Perhaps that describes your life or your giant now. Trust your group enough to share that life-altering experience. Allow them to pray for you and encourage you as you prepare to take the final steps to conquer your giant. You may need to forgive the person or persons responsible for this tragedy. Or you may need to forgive God. Take time with this question. It could be key to your victory. What would it take for you to develop a Caleb spirit?

GIANT KILLING STRATEGY RENEWING YOUR MIND

Most of us approach giant killing with an unrenewed mind. Years of failure have convinced us that we can never kill this giant. As the Israelite spies said, "We were like grasshoppers in our own sight, and so we were in their sight" (Numbers 13:33). We feel small and inadequate, so we rehearse smallness and inadequacy. The giant laughs, and we feel even less capable. I hope by now you've had at least some small gains. Even huge gains!

Now is the time to renew your mind (Romans 12:2) by taking every thought captive. My favorite passage to motivate this is 2 Corinthians 10:4-5. God will provide the weapons, but we have to use them.

As we discussed in Lesson 4, our giants form demonic strongholds in our minds. They loom large and impermeable. But the truth is, we have the weapons in the power of the Holy Spirit to shatter those strongholds. This strategy starts with identifying lies (strongholds, arguments, mindsets). We did this in Lesson 2. Now, let's take it a bit deeper. Identify the lie and write a statement that feels true to you ("I don't have a choice."). Then, cast down the argument by taking it deeper. "If I don't have a choice, then…" Go deeper. "If [your then] is true, then…." Allow yourself to go down the rabbit hole, preferably with a trusted friend. You will find that almost every final "then" is "Then I will die." Some people get there quickly; others take a while. But the reality is that a spirit of death is doing its best to get you to give up and die, or fade into nothingness.

Take your original thought and rephrase it to bring it into the knowledge of God and obedience to Christ. Choose a new mindset. Write it out. Speak it out loud. Over and over. Do battle with it like you did in Week 10. Every 37 seconds. Choose the NEW mindset that will propel you to victory over this and all your giants. You can see an example of how this works in Appendix B.

f.   Proverbs 13:12 says, *"Hope deferred makes the heart sick…"* Describe how hope deferred has affected your ability to conquer your giant. Just as Caleb insisted that Joshua give him the portion Moses promised him, petition God for your promised portion. (If this feels too bold or sacrilegious, read Isaiah 45:11.)

"Then the land had rest from war" (Joshua 14:15b). What beautiful words for a people who had come out of slavery in Egypt, had wandered 38 years in the wilderness, then had spent seven years battling giants. How they must have longed for a settled life, a life where they could plant fields and expect to eat the harvest.

11a. Describe your own spiritual journey—your slavery, your wandering, your battles, your rest. Where are you in the process now?

b.   What do you know for sure? (See Deuteronomy 31:6, Hebrews 13:5b).

After a lifetime of faithful obedience, Joshua accepted his transition without question. What an example this must have been to the nation! God grant that each of us can also develop such a consistent walk of faithful obedience that transition or change cannot threaten or upset us!

MEMORY VERSE: *Deuteronomy 31:6 (NIV)*
Be strong and of good courage, do not fear nor be afraid of them; for the LORD your God, He is the One who goes with you. He will not leave you nor forsake you.

Keys To Conquering My Giant From This Lesson

Consider how you can apply what you've learned in Week 12 as you finish conquering your giant.

ACTION ITEMS:

A.

B.

C.

Notes & Prayer Requests

WEEK 13
FINISHING WELL

How do you say goodbye to someone you've loved? How do you end a lifelong relationship? Saying farewell is always difficult, especially when it's a final parting from someone with whom you've shared a significant piece of life.

Joshua faced this task as he neared death. It was time to bid farewell to the nation. These were not just faceless settlers, but his friends, relatives, and co-workers. They were people with whom he had shared one of the great dramas of history.

What could he tell them to summarize his life and his commitment to the Lord? What did they need to remember after he was gone? What words might stay with them as reminders when the going got tough, when the temptations to stray from the Lord became overwhelming?

Joshua had served his nation well in life. His farewell prepared them for his death.

Getting Started

1. What is the most difficult farewell you have faced? What made it so difficult? How did you feel?

> *... parting is such sweet sorrow ...* [86]
> ~William Shakespeare

Background

Chapters 15-21 of Joshua describe the allocation of the land to the various tribes. This was done by lot, so the LORD was actually responsible for the division (rather than Joshua). In describing the allotments for many of the tribes, the author jumps ahead and tells how well they fared in claiming their inheritances. In many cases, they were not successful in totally routing out the Canaanites. (See Joshua 15:63, 16:10, and 17:12-13).

Joshua was still the encourager, the motivator, and the calmer of fears. When the descendants of Joseph complained they wanted more land (see Joshua 17:14-18), Matthew Henry reminds us, "Many wish for larger portions who do not cultivate and make the most of what they have."[87]

---

[86] William Shakespeare, *Romeo and Juliet, Act II, Scene ii.*
[87] Church, 232.

After moving the tabernacle to Shiloh[88] from its unguarded position at Gilgal (see Joshua 18:1), Joshua asked the tribes, "How long will you wait before you begin to take possession of the land that the LORD has given you?" (Joshua 18:3.) Living off the spoil of their enemies, they had already become slack and lazy.

2. What "lands" do you already have title to that you have been slack to occupy? (See 2 Peter 1:3-4). Is there an area in your life where you have asked for a larger portion when you have not yet been faithful to what you have already been given?

Joshua had the men from the remaining tribes survey the land and then continued the division by lot (see Joshua 18:4-19:48). Finally, at the insistence of the Israelites, Joshua received his inheritance in the hill country of his tribe, Ephraim (see Joshua 19:49-50). The town was not the best—it needed to be "built up" before it could be settled. This leader was not in a hurry, nor did he seek the best portion.

After Joshua received his portion, the cities of refuge were identified (see Joshua 20), and finally, the towns for the Levites were designated (see Joshua 21). The tribe of Levi was the priestly tribe and did not receive a separate inheritance. Rather, the LORD had determined that, since Levi served the entire nation in matters of worship, they should receive 48 cities scattered throughout the land (see Numbers 35:8). The Israelites gave them some of the best cities.

---

[88] Shiloh means *rest*. What more appropriate location as the land and the nation transitioned from war to rest.

Read Joshua 22

The armies and troops, including those from east of the Jordan, remained armed until the battles were over, and Joshua gave them permission to return to their homes (see Joshua 22:1-9). He gave them an honorable discharge, along with the spoils of their efforts. They had been faithful and obedient in helping their brothers win their land.

3a. What was Joshua's concern in Joshua 22:5? (See Deuteronomy 8:10-20).

b. Do you find it more difficult to serve the LORD in good times than in trials? If so, why? What specific steps can you take to increase your faithfulness and thankfulness in the good times?

c. As you conquer your giant, what temptations or challenges do you foresee? How can you prepare in advance to overcome those?

Upon their return to their lands, the two-and-a-half Eastern tribes built an imposing altar by the Jordan. This caused great concern among the tribes west of the Jordan, for the LORD had been very clear that the Israelites were to have only one place of worship (as opposed to the many held by the pagans—Deuteronomy 12:1-14). The Western tribes immediately assembled and sent a delegate from each tribe to confront the Eastern tribes. They were concerned not only for the Eastern tribes but also for the entire community, for the Lord had made it clear that they were to be responsible for one another. They still remembered His wrath concerning Achan's disobedience.

> *Our relationship with other believers must be characterized by open, honest communication and by trust.*

The Eastern tribes responded immediately that they had no intention of setting up another place of worship. Rather, they were concerned that their descendants would be turned away from the true place of worship by those who would say that the Jordan was the boundary. They had established this new altar as a witness between themselves and the Western tribes.

Although Joshua is not mentioned in this chapter, his excellent leadership is apparent. The people have learned from him. The way the elders handled the response of the two-and-a-half tribes is also important. After listening to the representatives of the Eastern tribes, the Western leaders:

- Did not question their sincerity.
- Did not criticize them for their rash and perhaps inadvisable action.
- Did not fish for evidence to prove their charge.
- Did not continue to press the issue.

A lot of personal misunderstandings and church hurt and could be avoided if we all followed this pattern.

4a. When faced with a similar situation, what is your tendency? Are you more likely to react as these elders did or to react with the negative side of one or more of the attitudes above?

b. If the latter, what might be the root cause? What would be a better response? (See James 1:19-20).

Many years passed between chapters 22 and 23—historians suggest about 18. The Israelites had settled in the land and had begun to enjoy—perhaps even take for granted—their inheritance. They had built cities and planted crops. Children had been born, and elders had died. Life seemed pretty normal.

Joshua had remained faithful to the Lord, and through his leadership and example, so had the nation. But temptations permeated their society (as they do all societies). The Canaanites were not yet destroyed in some areas. In fact, where they were only subdued, they were an even greater threat to the values and morals of the nation as they lived peacefully as neighbors. As warring enemies, they had remained nameless. Horrible imaginations of their pagan practices helped maintain the distance.[89] But as neighbors, they became real people with names, real people "just like us." And real people with a religion that seemed perhaps more exciting, more intriguing than that of the Israelites.

---

[89] Remember the description of Canaanite religious practices in *Week 1, Preparing to Conquer.*

It was in this setting that Joshua gave his farewell, first to the leaders and then to all the tribes. Now "old and stricken in years," he had earned the right to be heard, for he had lived most of his life in their service.

Read Joshua 23

5a. Whom did Joshua credit with their successes, both past and future?

b. What warnings and encouragements did he give in verses 6-10? Why was this particularly important for this audience?

c. He also gave them a command in verse 11 we have seldom heard in this book. What was it?

d. Why would he encourage them to *love* the LORD rather than simply fear or obey Him? (See John 14:15, 1 John 4:18).

> *The most effective motivator for obedience is a deep and abiding love for our Lord Jesus Christ.*

e. Do you really *love* God, or do you obey Him simply because you fear Him? (See Revelation 2:4). What does love look like, in your opinion?

6a. What warnings did Joshua give in verses 12-13?

b. Is there an area in your life where you are "neighbors with the Canaanites?" An area where you so regularly see sin or idolatry that you hardly notice it? An area where, because of familiarity, you even slip on occasion? Describe it and your reaction to it.

c. How might that hinder the total conquering of your giant?

7a. What were the promises the LORD gave them which had not failed (See Deuteronomy 28:1-14)? What were some of the curses the LORD promised for disobedience (Deuteronomy 28:15-68)?

b. What does Deuteronomy 28 tell you about the seriousness with which God considers His command for obedience? Given the options, are you choosing obedience or disobedience?

c. From your knowledge of the Old Testament, what did the Israelites choose?

Spiritual compromise is a gradual and insidious process. Israel's greatest danger was not military. It was moral and spiritual.[90]
~Donald Campbell

---
[90] Campbell.

> ## GIANT KILLING STRATEGY
> ## SABBATH
>
> On the seventh day of creation, God rested. Not because He was tired, but because He knew when to stop. When to say, "Enough."
>
> One of the problems with people engaged in giant killing is that we don't know when to stop. We don't know when to rest. We drive ourselves like slaves. We get exhausted and keep going. And then in desperation, we quit.
>
> If you haven't done so yet, take a Sabbath. Pause. Rest. Breathe. What remains of your giant will still be there tomorrow. God calls us to stop and devote 24 hours to Him. Those who do so can attest of the importance of this practice. It gives both the mind and the body an opportunity to stop, to rest, and to be refreshed.
>
> What does that look like? Spend time with friends and family. Celebrate. Create art or music. Eat good food. Read good books. Avoid screens as much as possible. Pray. Meditate. Cease striving. Fall in love with God all over again. REST.

Read Joshua 24

Having addressed the elders, Joshua now assembled all the tribes—the ordinary people. The address to the elders was fitting for them—strong admonitions against serving other gods and encouragement for them as leaders. His address to the people, by contrast, was mostly a historical reminder of God's faithfulness.

The meeting was held at Shechem rather than Shiloh, perhaps because it was closer to Joshua's home. This was also the place where Abraham had settled when he came to Canaan and where God had appeared to him (see Genesis 12:6-7). It was also near Mts. Ebal and Gerizim, where the people had renewed their covenant when they entered the land.

Now, they were called to renew the covenant again. Chapter 24 reads like the typical vassal covenant Moses had originally administered before his death, and the one made when the people entered the land.

Now Joshua spoke the word of the LORD to them as a prophet and reminded them again of God's great faithfulness to them. He retold the history of the nation, ending in the present tense—they *are* living in a land on which they did not toil, and in cities which they did not build, and *are* eating from vineyards they did not plant. This was a reminder of God's promise to them in Deuteronomy 6:10-11.

8a. What does verse Joshua 24:14 imply?

b. Why does it seem as if God alone is never sufficient? Why are we so prone to violate the second commandment (see Exodus 20:4)?

c. Of course, today, we are too sophisticated to carve and worship wooden idols, but we still set up false gods nonetheless. What are some of the other gods you trust in? A few are listed below. Feel free to add your own. What does this say about your faith?

Sex	Money	
Power	Job or career	
Education	Ministry	
Family (especially children)	"Professionals" (doctors, ministers, scientists, politicians)	
Reputation	Respect	
Freedom	License	

d. How might these idols be hindering the conquering of your giant?

9a. What is Joshua's point in verse 15?

b. Who or what do you *choose* to serve? What does that mean you must forsake? Are you willing to do that?

> The choice is clear. Serving the LORD brings life; serving other gods brings death. Knowing this, why do we continue to vacillate? Many years later, another prophet asked the Israelites the same question:
>
> *"Elijah went before the people and said, 'How long will you waver between two opinions? If the Lord is God, follow Him; but if Baal is God, follow him.'"*
>
> ~1 Kings 18:21

10a. What choice did the Israelites make before Joshua?

b. Knowing that he will no longer be there to monitor, encourage, or chasten them, what does Joshua do?

Every covenant or agreement needs witnesses to be legal. In this case, both the people and the stone monument were witnesses to the covenant. When Israel broke the covenant later, the LORD could point to this moment and the agreement it represented to justify his punishment.

c. How can serving as a "witness against" one another help maintain obedience?

d. Do you need others to help you remain strong and obedient? Why?

We need community. We need one another. We need to be willing to encourage one another, to walk alongside one another, to teach and admonish one another. We need to covenant not only with God but also with one another.

11. Take time to summarize your progression in conquering your giant. In what ways do you look more like Jesus than you did 12 weeks ago? What have you learned along the way? What remains to be done? What is your plan to finish well?

IMPORTANT ASSIGNMENT: Find at least one person with whom you can covenant to continue practicing what you have learned in this study. Determine now to meet and pray together regularly. Agree to be accountable to one another before God for both your actions and your thoughts for some period after this group ends. This is especially important if you are still struggling with aspects of your giant. And it's equally important if you have conquered the giant as you strive to maintain the victory.

Joshua, an ordinary man, had served his LORD in extraordinary ways through a life of faithful obedience. He had indeed conquered giants in the power and under the direction of the LORD his God. Now, as he faced his final rest, he surely heard the words, "Well done, good and faithful servant! You have been faithful with a few things; I will put you in charge of many things. Come and share your master's happiness!" (Matthew 25:21).

May each of us determine to live our lives in such faithful obedience that we will indeed live **EXTRAORDINARY** lives for our LORD, Jesus Christ.

> *Being a child of God has always been a*
> *serious business.*
> *It is not something one can do in his*
> *spare time as a hobby.*
> *Yahweh demands of His people nothing less than complete*
> *dedication, unwavering loyalty.*[91]
> *~William C. Martin*

MEMORY VERSE: *Joshua 24:15*
And if it seems evil to you to serve the LORD, choose for yourselves this day whom you will serve, whether the gods which your fathers served that were on the other side of the River, or the gods of the Amorites, in whose land you dwell. **But as for me and my house, we will serve the LORD.**

---

[91] William C. Martin, M.A., B.D., *These Were God's People: A Bible History* (Nashville, Tenn.: The Southwestern Company, 1966), 93.

Keys To Conquering My Giant From This Lesson

Consider how you can apply what you've learned in Week 13 as you begin to conquer your giant.

ACTION ITEMS:

A.

B.

C.

Notes & Prayer Requests

APPENDIX A
FEARS THAT CONQUER ME

As you go through this list, listen to the Holy Spirit. Clothe yourself with the armor of God and tell God that you want to hear only HIS truth. Do not allow these words to stir up more fear, but if you get a memory of something that caused this fear, write down what you remember and what is stirred up. These words have no power over you.

- Some of these are actual fears, and others are behaviors that result from the fear. Both are important to understanding what harms you.
- Circle the number that most closely resembles the fear you have of this item. Don't think too much about this. Just do it.
- If you are reminded of a sin, confess it and receive God's grace.
- If you sense bitterness or unforgiveness, stop and forgive the person and release him or her from all bitterness and judgment.
- If you think of a fear not listed, add it to the right category.

TYPE OF FEAR	LEAST MOST
FEAR OF MAN	
• Fear of family members (Who?)	1 2 3 4 5 6 7 8 9 10
• Fear of being wrong	1 2 3 4 5 6 7 8 9 10
• Need to control others	1 2 3 4 5 6 7 8 9 10
• Distrust	1 2 3 4 5 6 7 8 9 10
• Fear of another's feelings	1 2 3 4 5 6 7 8 9 10
• Fear of another's words or actions	1 2 3 4 5 6 7 8 9 10
• Fear of authority	1 2 3 4 5 6 7 8 9 10
• Fear of being controlled	1 2 3 4 5 6 7 8 9 10
• Fear of betrayal	1 2 3 4 5 6 7 8 9 10
• Fear of bigotry, prejudice, or racism	1 2 3 4 5 6 7 8 9 10
• Fear of criticism	1 2 3 4 5 6 7 8 9 10
• Fear of disapproval	1 2 3 4 5 6 7 8 9 10
FEAR OF REJECTION	
• Fear of another's bitterness	1 2 3 4 5 6 7 8 9 10
• Fear of being shamed	1 2 3 4 5 6 7 8 9 10

TYPE OF FEAR	LEAST MOST
FEAR OF FAILURE	
• Fear of challenges	1 2 3 4 5 6 7 8 9 10
• Fear of worst case (what if)	1 2 3 4 5 6 7 8 9 10
• Fear of the past (if only)	1 2 3 4 5 6 7 8 9 10
• Fear of a wasted life	1 2 3 4 5 6 7 8 9 10
• Drivenness	1 2 3 4 5 6 7 8 9 10
FEAR OF SUCCESS	
• Fear of moving forward, taking reasonable risks	1 2 3 4 5 6 7 8 9 10
• Fear of opportunity	1 2 3 4 5 6 7 8 9 10
• Drivenness	1 2 3 4 5 6 7 8 9 10
• Fear of being free	1 2 3 4 5 6 7 8 9 10
• Fear of deliverance, freedom	1 2 3 4 5 6 7 8 9 10
FEAR OF ABANDONMENT	
• Fear of being abandoned	1 2 3 4 5 6 7 8 9 10
• Fear of abandoning others	1 2 3 4 5 6 7 8 9 10
• Fear of dependency	1 2 3 4 5 6 7 8 9 10

TYPE OF FEAR	LEAST MOST
FEAR OF DANGER	
• Fear of attack, rape	1 2 3 4 5 6 7 8 9 10
• Fear of war, violence	1 2 3 4 5 6 7 8 9 10
• Fear of catastrophe	1 2 3 4 5 6 7 8 9 10
• Fear of earthquakes	1 2 3 4 5 6 7 8 9 10
• Fear of flood	1 2 3 4 5 6 7 8 9 10
• Fear of the future	1 2 3 4 5 6 7 8 9 10
• Fear of robbery or losing possessions	1 2 3 4 5 6 7 8 9 10
• Fear of death	1 2 3 4 5 6 7 8 9 10
• Fear of disability	1 2 3 4 5 6 7 8 9 10
FEAR OF TANGIBLE THINGS	
• Animals	1 2 3 4 5 6 7 8 9 10
• Blood	1 2 3 4 5 6 7 8 9 10
• Disease or illness	1 2 3 4 5 6 7 8 9 10
• Buildings	1 2 3 4 5 6 7 8 9 10
• Elevators	1 2 3 4 5 6 7 8 9 10
• Stairwells	1 2 3 4 5 6 7 8 9 10
• Men or women	1 2 3 4 5 6 7 8 9 10
• Clowns	1 2 3 4 5 6 7 8 9 10

TYPE OF FEAR	Least　　　　　　　　　　　Most
FEAR OF INTANGIBLE THINGS	
• Fear of bad news	1 2 3 4 5 6 7 8 9 10
• Fear of the dark or dark places	1 2 3 4 5 6 7 8 9 10
• Fear of change	1 2 3 4 5 6 7 8 9 10
• Fear of commitment	1 2 3 4 5 6 7 8 9 10
RANDOM ANXIETY AND STRESS	
• Distress	1 2 3 4 5 6 7 8 9 10
• Fear of being alone	1 2 3 4 5 6 7 8 9 10

Look at your list. Calculating a total is less important than just identifying and acknowledging your greatest fears. Keep these in mind as you go through this Bible study. Come back when you finish and see if any of your scores are different.

APPENDIX B
TRANSFORMING NEGATIVE THOUGHTS (TNT)™

In Week 12, we introduced the *Giant Killing Strategy* of Renewing the Mind and suggested a technique for addressing the deeper issues driving you. This Appendix will provide a bit more information and show you how to transform negative thoughts—for yourself or with a friend.

It is a well-known fact among cognitive behavioral therapists that while our emotions *should not* be the drivers of our actions, many people *are* governed by their feelings. They *feel* as if they must cater to every emotion. They *feel* as if they don't have a choice. This results in destructive behaviors and more negative emotions. Letting your emotions rule is like giving a three-year-old the keys to the car.

The truth is, emotions are simply indicators that something is amiss in your thought life. The truth is that our feelings and subsequent behaviors are the result of what we *think* or *believe*. Proverbs 23:7 tells us, "For as he thinks in his heart, so is he." This is why Paul tells us in Romans 12:2 that we can be transformed (changed) by the renewing of our minds. Not our emotions or behaviors. When we change what we *think*, we change how we feel and how we behave.

All of us have beliefs that are based on lies. And the fruit of believing those lies is sin, which leads to death (see Romans 6:23). Therefore, to heal and thrive, we must change the way we *think*. The most effective way to do that is to identify the lie and then change that wrong or ungodly belief into a truth. Let's look at how we do that.

A common lie is, "I don't have a choice." We use this as an excuse for almost anything. It's an excuse as ancient as humankind. Remember the story of the Fall?

> "Then the man said, 'The woman whom You gave to be with me, she gave me of the tree, and I ate.' And the LORD God said to the woman, 'What is this you have done?' The woman said, 'The serpent deceived me, and I ate.'" (Adam and Eve in Genesis 3:12-13, explaining why they didn't have a choice to eat the fruit.)

We see the same lie in Exodus when Aaron made a golden calf for the Israelites to worship:

> "And I said to them, 'Whoever has any gold, let them break it off.' So they gave it to me, and I cast it into the fire, and this calf came out" (Exodus 32:24).

We do the same thing, convincing ourselves and trying to convince others that we don't have a choice:

- I drink (smoke, take drugs, eat too much) because I don't have a choice. (I can't stop. I need it. I don't have any power over it.)
- I took that job (stay in that job) because I didn't have a choice. That's why I'm miserable.

The Truth is, we always have a choice—not necessarily a good choice, not necessarily one we *want*, but a choice. So, how do we get through the lie and find the truth?

Mary is a woman in your group who has been unemployed for months. This is her giant. She needs a job—badly. She's been offered a job but feels it's not "just right," so she's waffling on whether to take it or not. Randy is helping her think through her beliefs so she can identify the lies, determine the truth, and transform her negative emotions.

Randy: "What's the obstacle to your taking this job?

Mary: "Well, it just doesn't fit what I'm looking for, but I feel I don't have a choice. I must take it, and I don't want to."

Randy: "Why don't you have a choice?"

Mary: "Because if I don't take this one, I may never get another offer." [*Look for "always" and "never." They are sure signs of a lie.*]

Randy: "And if you never get another offer?"

Mary: "Well, I'll be just like I am now. Broke!"

Randy: "And if you're broke like now?" [*Just follow the person's line of reasoning. Let them lead you. Sometimes it will go fast. Other times they will meander a bit. But let them lead you.*]

Mary: "Then I won't be able to pay my rent!"

Randy: "And if you can't pay your rent?"

Mary: "I'll be evicted."

Randy: "And if you're evicted?"

Mary: "I'll be homeless."

Randy: "And if you're homeless?"

Mary: "Then I'll be out on the street and that will be dangerous and awful!"

Randy: "And if you're out on the dangerous, awful street?"

Mary: "Then I'll be vulnerable, and something awful will happen to me."

Randy: "And if something awful happens to you?"

Mary: "Then I'll die!"

Regardless of the initial lie, if we follow the internal reasoning, the result is almost always death or oblivion. It's utterly uncanny! Most people have a deep-seated fear of death hidden under piles of lies, excuses, and emotions. This fear is less of dying than of oblivion, of being even less important than they feel they already are. Once we identify that and realize how unlikely that scenario is, it's easier to think more clearly, get to the truth, and adopt a mindset that will help rather than hinder.

This fear of dying or oblivion also usually lacks God. The person feels all alone, usually very little, and incapable of seeing the truth. If we bring God and His Truth into the discussion, the person is no longer all alone and little. With God in the discussion, they can make better decisions and, in this case, see that no choice is forever.

In Mary's case, the thought of taking a less-than-perfect job *feels* like death and danger, a dead-end. It feels like there is no good choice, that she's being forced into something awful forever. Thus, the catastrophic spiral.

If Mary can change her thoughts and her belief system to something more truthful, she will be able to make a better decision. She might decide, "While this job isn't perfect, it is a job that I am capable of doing, and it will solve my immediate need for income. I will accept this job and keep looking for something better suited to me, confident that God won't leave me there forever." As she begins to rehearse this new belief, the fear of the doom-filled unknown decreases, and she is able to approach her giant with a more clear mind.

Or, she might decide, "Regardless of how badly I need a job, this one simply will not work for me. I will turn it down and keep looking, confident that God has a better solution for me." Depending on many factors, this may or may not be a good decision. But it is a decision that will keep her moving forward in faith rather than stuck in her emotions.

Either way, she learns she has a choice. It might be helpful for Randy to help her try on both of those mindsets and see which one best fits her. One will usually feel like a comfortable fit, or at least something she can live with. Neither is permanent. Both can be changed. But choosing one of them will help her move forward governed by truth rather than fear or lies.

BIBLIOGRAPHY

———. *Expositor's Bible Commentary Abridged Edition—Two Volume Set (NIV Commentary)*. 1,6 vols., edited by Kenneth Baker, and John R. Kohlenberger III (Consulting Editors). Grand Rapids, MI: Zondervan, 1994.

———. *A Navpress Bible Study on the Book of Joshua*. Colorado Springs, CO: NavPress, 1988.

———. *The NET Bible Second Edition Notes (NET Notes)*. Second Edition Notes (NET Notes) ed. Nashville, TN: Thomas Nelson, 2019. 5.8. OakTree Software, Inc.

———. *Preaching the Word Commentary*. Accordance edition hypertexted and formatted by OakTree Software, Inc., Version 1.5 ed. Wheaton, Illinois: Crossway Books.

(Firm), NavPress. *A Life-Changing Encounter with God's Word from the Book of Joshua*. Colorado Springs: NavPress, 1988.

Baker, Kenneth and John R. Kohlenberger III (Consulting Editors), ed., *Expositor's Bible Commentary Abridged Edition-Two Volume Set (NIV Commentary)*. Grand Rapids, MI: Zondervan, 1994.

Becher, Rabbi Mordechai "History of Events of Tisha B'av." Accessed 2023_12_13, 2023. https://ohr.edu/1088

Bonhoeffer, D., and E. Metaxas. *The Cost of Discipleship*: Touchstone, 2012.

Calvin, John. *Commentary on the Book of Psalms*. Translated by James Anderson. Vol. 2, 1845.

Campbell, Donald K. *Joshua, Leader under Fire*. Wheaton, IL: Victor Books, 1986.

Church, Leslie F., F.R.Hist.S, ed., *Commentary on the Whole Bible by Matthew Henry*. Grand Rapids, Mich: Zondervan Publishing House, 1961.

Edersheim, Alfred. *Old Testament Bible History*. Wilmington, Del: Associated Publishers and Authors.

Fulghum, Robert. *All I Really Need to Know I Learned in Kindergarten*. 15th anniversary ed. New York: Ballantine Books, 2003.

Hansel, Tim. *Ya' Gotta Keep Dancin'*. Elgin, Ill.: David C. Cook Publishing Company, 1985.

Jamison, Robert, Fausset, A.R., and David Brown. *Jamison Fausset and Brown's Commendary Critical and Explanatory on the Whole Bible*: Accordance Bible Software, Oaktree Software, Inc., 1871. 2.6.

Jensen, Irving L. *Joshua: Rest-Land Won. Everyman's Bible Commentary*. Chicago, IL: Moody Press, 1966.

Keller, W. Phillip. *Joshua : Mighty Warrior and Man of Faith*. Grand Rapids, Mich.: Kregel Publications, 1992.

Martin, William C., M.A., B.D. *These Were God's People: A Bible History*. Nashville, Tenn.: The Southwestern Company, 1966.

McCraty, Rollin Ph.D., Mike Atkinson, Dana Tomasino, B.A., and William A. Tiller, Ph.D. "The Electricity of Touch: Detection and Measurement of Cardiac Energy Exchange between People." 1998.

Seevers, Boyd. *Warfare in the Old Testament: The Organization, Weapons, and Tactics of Ancient near Eastern Armies*: Kregel Academic, 2013.

Sheehy, Gail. *Passages : Predictable Crises of Adult Life*. Ballantine Books Trade pbk. ed. New York: Ballantine Books, 2006.

Solomon, Marty. "Knowing When to Say 'Enough'." Season 1, Episode 2. in *BEMA Podcast*. https://www.bemadiscipleship.com/2

Swiggum, Harley. *The Bethel Bible Series: Old Testament*. Madison, Wisconsin: The Adult Christian Education Foundation, 1961, 1981.

Tiegreen, Chris. *Heaven on Earth*: Tyndale, 2015.

Tozer, A.W. *The Root of the Righteous*. Harrisburg, PA: Christian Publications, 1955.

Wiersbe, Warren W., and Thomas Nelson Publishers. *The Essential Everyday Bible Commentary: With the Complete Text of the New King James Version*. Nashville: T. Nelson, 1993.

Other Books by Pat J. Sikora

You can see all of Pat's books & artwork at www.PatSikora.com/Shop

www.ingramcontent.com/pod-product-compliance
Lightning Source LLC
Chambersburg PA
CBHW081442070526
44586CB00019B/2204